THE
LITTLE
BOOK
OF
DERRY

CATHAL MCGUIGAN

The History Press Ireland

First published 2015
This paperback edition published 2019

The History Press
97 St George's Place
Cheltenham
GL50 3QB
www.thehistorypress.ie

British Library Cataloguing in Publication Data.
A catalogue record for this book is available from the British Library.

978 0 7509 9234 3
Typesetting and origination by The History Press

Printed and bound by TJ International Ltd

CONTENTS

ACKNOWLEDGEMENTS

CATHAL MCGUIGAN

I would like to offer a big thank you to Libraries NI, who have great facilities and warm-hearted staff across Northern Ireland. Their online resources were also extremely useful, particularly the ability to access the Lexis Nexis newspaper database.

Thanks to Beth Amphlett and Ronan Colgan from The History Press Ireland for giving me the opportunity to write this book and for all their help and patience.

Thanks to Adam Kee for his outstanding illustrations, good humour and precision, and to my friends and family for their help and support.

ADAM KEE

Thanks to my wife Michelle for her support and to my children Farren and Merryn for their honesty towards my drawings! Thanks also to Cathal for trusting me.

INTRODUCTION

Derry has many names, more than your average county or city, yet they all begin with Doire, the Irish word for oak wood or oak grove. The image is fitting for an area that is at once ancient and familiar, serene and wild, and emerging from a difficult past into a promising future.

This book aims to cover all of the major events, people and tales of County Derry and Derry city, but in its roots it is a little book. Although it speaks of the Siege and the Troubles and the great men and women, *The Little Book of Derry* is also a book of fragments and quiet things that may not appear in the grand narrative of the place.

It is well known in Derry that greatness can grow from the most modest of places. The son of a Limavady farmer, William Massey, can move to the other side of the globe and stand shoulder to shoulder with world leaders, as the Prime Minister of New Zealand. The son of a Bellaghy farmer can captivate the world with Derry's landscapes, characters and sounds and speak with strength among the titans of literature.

In Derry we know that 'acting the eejit' is not always stupid and without purpose. One flighty Ballinascreen man, Hudy McGuigan, strapped wings made from doors to his arms and jumped off a cliff. He must have gone at least a few feet before he tumbled into a thorn bush. Nearly a century later another man tested out an early aeroplane on Magilligan strand, reaching heights of 40 feet. Within thirty years, a woman touched down just outside Derry as a record holder, having crossed the Atlantic alone after fifteen hours in a plane. Was Hudy simple, or just ahead of his time?

This book is a snapshot of what it means to be of Derry, an attempt to capture its essence in amber.

Derry is a place where the voices of farmers' sons can be voices that inspire and enchant the world. It is a place where people dare to fly and look foolish rather than stay grounded and hushed.

Humble beginnings are no obstacle here. No matter how many Derry folk grow powerful or magnificent and whatever dizzy heights they reach, there are always more acorns in the oak grove.

And mighty oaks from little acorns grow.

1

HISTORY

The story of the people and places of Derry city and county begins near Coleraine in 7000 BC, with some of the earliest settlers in Ireland. It is typical of the area that its inhabitants are ahead of their time. Over the years, Derry has been a site of religious importance, a fiercely contested battleground and the departure point for pioneers that would shape America, Canada and beyond.

Here we look over the 9,000-year history of Derry, a tale of poetry and protest, industry and innovation, warfare and wonder.

MAJOR EVENTS

c. 7900 BC-7600 BC	The Mesolithic Age – The earliest known settlement of people in Ireland is at Mountsandel near Coleraine.
c. 4500 BC-2500 BC	The Neolithic Age – The population of Ireland begins to grow as agriculture develops. Contact begins with traders from mainland Europe and Britain, allowing farmers to bring domesticated cattle and sheep to Ireland.
	Flint artefacts and evidence of buildings dated to around 3000 BC were found in Killane when excavations were carried out for the Limavady bypass in 2002. Megalithic burial tombs, found across Derry and Ireland, also date from this period.
c. 2500 BC-700 BC	The Bronze Age – Metalworking begins in Ireland, which allows inhabitants to create better tools

and weapons but also early metal instruments like horns made of brass. Gold is plentiful, allowing the creation of elaborate jewellery.

c. 700 BC The Iron Age – Celts arrive in Ulster, bringing iron weapons. They trade, fight and integrate with the natives. Successive waves of Celtic invaders continue to arrive until around 100 BC.

c. 100 BC Artefacts that make up the Broighter Hoard – found near Limavady in 1896 – indicate that the locals were skilled in creating impressive gold artefacts.

AD 89 The Roman historian Tacitus speaks of a warrior called Galgacus leading the Celts into battle against Romans in Scotland. This may be a reference to Calgach after whom one of the area's earliest settlements, Doire Calgach, is named.

AD 140 Ptolemy's map of Ireland makes reference to Derry's rivers. He calls them the Widwa (Foyle) and the Argita (Bann). He names the people of the area Wenniknioi or Rhobogdioi. At this time the Irish are exposed to Roman thought and technology through trade with Britain. Kings and tribes across Ireland battle for dominance.

AD 521 Believed date that Derry's patron saint, Columba, was born in Gartan, County Donegal.

AD 546 Columba said to have originally founded Derry city and built a monastery on the bank of the Foyle. Christianity is relatively new in Ireland after much resistance from the dominant pagan faith of the Druids.

AD 790-1014 The Vikings invade Ireland, raiding sporadically at first. The Irish engage them in battle when they come in larger numbers. In 833 an Irish force managed to defeat invading Vikings in Derry. Aed Findliath, the High King of Ireland, also won a major naval battle on Lough Foyle in the 860s. Following the

Battle of Clontarf in 1014, the Vikings lose much of their power. Their influence can still be seen today in certain surnames commonly found in Derry, like McLaughlin and McGuigan.

1164	Tempall Mór, the 'great church', is erected by a successor of Colmcille. The parish Templemore would take its name from this church.
1170	The English earl Richard de Clare, known as Strongbow, arrives with a force in Ireland, a major event in the Norman invasion of Ireland. His success draws the attention of Henry II, who soon invades and establishes control over Ireland. Successive English kings have an influence on Irish culture, customs and laws.
1311	Richard de Burgo, the Earl of Ulster, is granted lands in Derry by Edward II.
1315	Edward the Bruce lands in Ulster with a large Scottish army, seeking to win Ireland's independence from England. He is supported by Irish chiefs, including some O'Cahans. After some early successes and a brief visit from his brother Robert, Edward is defeated near Dundalk in 1318. Famine devastates Europe around this time, killing an estimated 10-25 per cent of the Irish population.
1367	The Statutes of Kilkenny are enacted. Their aim is to stop English settlers mixing with the Irish, speaking the Irish language or taking part in Irish customs.
1449	King Henry VI sends Richard Plantagenet to Ireland. Chieftains in Ulster and Leinster submit to him. Richard's power grows, angering the king. His actions in Ireland influence the War of the Roses.
1535	Henry VIII is declared the head of the Church of Ireland. Catholics are caught between their loyalty to the Pope and being considered traitors to the crown.

1560	Shane O'Neill wants to inherit the title of Earl of Tyrone but does not fully recognise the authority of Elizabeth I. English armies arrive in Ulster, under the command of Sir Henry Sidney, and a series of battles follow.
1566	A fleet under the command of Edward Randolph lands at Derry. He makes camp and builds defences.
1567	A fire destroys the settlement. It spreads to the gunpowder store, causing a huge explosion.
1585	County Coleraine (sometimes spelt Colerain) is established by John Perrot, the Lord Deputy of Ireland.
1588	The Spanish Armada arrives. The shipwreck of *La Trinidad Valencera*, which sank off Donegal was later recovered by the City of Derry Sub Aqua Club in 1971 and can now be seen in The Tower Museum.

1594-1603	The Nine Year's War between Hugh O'Neill and the forces of Elizabeth I.
1600	Henry Docwra sails into Lough Foyle with over 4,000 men and captures Derry. He plans to wait out the winter, but the weather takes a great toll on his troops. The following year his forces raid and pillage the local area, killing many peasants. He founds a new English settlement at Derry.

1604	Derry becomes the first city in Ulster when it is awarded a royal charter by James I.
1605	The Protestant Church in Ireland banishes Catholic priests and makes attendance at Protestant service compulsory.
1606	Docwra leaves Derry, leaving Sir George Paulett as governor.
1607	The Flight of the Earls sees O'Neill and his followers flee Ireland to mainland Europe. The property of the earls is declared the property of the Crown. It is to be divided up for plantations.
1608	Cahir O'Doherty's rebellion leads to the Burning of Derry, where the infant city is mostly destroyed.
1609	London merchants are approached with an opportunity to 'plant' the county on the Foyle's west bank.
1613	County Londonderry is created when James I gives a Royal Charter to the Irish Society to allow the county's plantation. The new city of Derry is created on the Foyle's west bank, opposite the ruins of 'old' Derry. The London livery companies settle here and the town grows quickly.
1633	Construction of St Columb's Cathedral is completed.
1641	Rebellion breaks out across Ulster, resulting in the massacre of many Protestant settlers.
1649-1650	Oliver Cromwell's time in Ireland is remembered for the brutality of his troops and their hatred of Catholics.
1649	The first Siege of Derry.
1688	November – The Williamite Wars begin between Catholic James II and the Protestant William of Orange.

	December – An army supporting James is refused entry to Derry. The famous siege begins. This would continue until July 1689 when a fleet arrives to relieves the city. Derry earns the title 'The Maiden City' as the walls were not breached.
1690	James is defeated at the Battle of the Boyne and flees to France.
1691	The Battle of Aughrim takes place in County Galway and decides the conflict once and for all, in favour of William of Orange.
1714	The Apprentice Boys of Derry founded.
1724	Bishop George Berkeley is appointed Dean of Derry.
1725	Cicily Jackson is burned at the stake on St Patrick's Day.
1739-1741	Potato famine in Ireland leads to widespread starvation and disease.
1772	The *Londonderry Journal* (now *Derry Journal*) is founded.
1791	A bridge across the Foyle is opened.
1795	The Orange Order is founded.
1798	The United Irishmen rebel and occupy towns and cities across Ireland. The British swiftly put down the rebellion. Most of the leadership is executed. Wolfe Tone died from wounds that may have been self-inflicted.
1801	The Act of Union comes into force.
1803	Robert Emmet attempts a rebellion by attacking Dublin Castle. It lasts less than a month. Emmet is hanged at Kilmainham Gaol.

1813	The Battle of Garvagh. Four hundred Catholic 'Ribbonmen' attempt to destroy a tavern where Orangemen meet. The Protestants were prepared for the attack and their muskets made light work of the poorly armed Ribbonmen, who fled.
1827	Magilligan Strand is used as the baseline for the Ordnance Survey of Ireland. The rest of the island is measured and mapped in reference to this line.
1829	Catholics are emancipated thanks to the efforts of Daniel O'Connell and his Catholic Association. O'Connell worked to repeal the Act of Union for the next two decades, but was unsuccessful.
	The owners of the *Londonderry Journal* change the paper's editorial policy to endorse Catholic Emancipation. William Wallen, the paper's editor, resigns and founds the *Londonderry Sentinel*.
1830	Ribbonmen and Orangemen clash at 12 July parades in Castledawson and Maghera. Several Catholic homes are burned as a result of the violence.
	Austin's Department Store opens in the Diamond.
1831	The Scott family begin exporting shirts to Glasgow, kicking off a thriving industry for Derry city.
1832	The Apprentice Boys burn an effigy of siege traitor Robert Lundy for the first time. This tradition continues today.
1839	*Oiche na Gaoithe Móire* – The Night of the Big Wind – A tremendous storm hits Ireland, bringing winds of over 115mph. Many people believe it is the end of the world.
1842	A public holiday is declared on 23 June and 20,000 people attend the launch of the world's largest screw-propelled ship, the *Great Northern*, in Derry.

1845-1851	*An Gorta Mór* – the Great Famine – brings much suffering to the people of Derry.

1848	John Mitchel, born near Dungiven, is deported to Australia with other leaders of the Young Irelanders for inciting rebellion. The remaining leaders stage a farcical battle later dubbed the 'battle of Widow McCormack's cabbage patch'.
1855	The railway between Derry and Belfast is opened.
1863	The Carlisle Bridge, made of iron, is built to replace the existing timber bridge over the Foyle.
1865	Magee College opened as a theological college. Florence Nightingale visits soon afterwards.
1869	Three die in riots when Queen Victoria's son, Arthur, visits the city.
1884	The Gaelic Athletic Association (GAA) is founded by Michael Cusack.

1890	The Guildhall is built.
1911-1916	Serial killer John Bodkin Adams attends Coleraine Academical Institution.
1912	William Massey, from Limavady, becomes Prime Minister of New Zealand.
	The present Guildhall is opened as the original was destroyed in a fire.
	The Home Rule Bill is passed in parliament, creating an independent Irish parliament. The Bill was to be enacted in 1914, but was postponed until the end of the First World War.
1914	The long fight for Home Rule ends. A new Irish parliament can now run most of the country's affairs.
1914-1918	Men from across Derry enlist to fight in the First World War. Some 5,000 are estimated to have volunteered from Derry city. Memorials to the fallen are erected in the city and towns across the county.
1916	The Easter Rising takes place in Dublin. The British brutally put down the rebellion and execute fourteen of the leaders behind the uprising.
1919-1921	The Irish War of Independence is fought between British forces and the IRA employing guerrilla tactics. The Black and Tans, a reserve force of the Royal Irish Constabulary, are ruthless and commit many atrocities during the conflict.
1921	British and Irish leaders sign the Anglo-Irish Treaty leading to the partition of Ireland. Derry becomes part of the new state of Northern Ireland. The border with Donegal is less than four miles from Derry city and the split separates families, friends and work colleagues.

1922-1923	The Irish Civil War is fought between those in favour of accepting the Treaty and those who want to fight on for the partitioned six counties.
1932	Amelia Earhart lands in a field at Ballyarnett having successfully flown across the Atlantic.
1933	The Craigavon Bridge is opened, replacing the Carlisle Bridge.
	Fascist General Italo Balbo, said to be Mussolini's right-hand man, arrived in Derry with an 'armada' of twenty-four seaplanes. The visit is mainly part of a propaganda stunt during the general's journey to the US.
1942	The United States Navy establish their first European base in Derry.
1945	German U-boats surrender at Lisahally.
1967	Northern Ireland Civil Rights Association (NICRA) is formed.
1968	New University of Ulster founded in Coleraine.
1969	The Battle of the Bogside. Student activists are attacked at Burntollet Bridge during a march.
1971	August – Internment is introduced in Northern Ireland.
	September – 14-year-old Annette McGavigan is shot dead by British soldiers. She was the first child to die in the conflict.
1972	January – Bloody Sunday – British soldiers open fire on people taking part in a NICRA rally. Thirteen men were killed, while others are seriously injured. The Widgery Inquiry into the shootings causes anger as it suggests that some victims were armed and that the soldiers returned fire and did not initiate the attack. Violence intensifies in Northern Ireland as a result.

March – Northern Ireland's government is suspended and direct rule from London is enacted.

July – Three car bombs planted by the IRA explode in Claudy killing nine civilians, including William Temple (16), Patrick Connolly (15) and Kathryn Eakin (8).

1973

June – Two cars bombs planted by the Provisional IRA explode in Coleraine. The first bomb killed six Protestant pensioners and injured thirty-three other people. No one is injured by the second bomb.

1982

December – The INLA plant a bomb at the Droppin Well bar in Ballykelly. The explosion causes the roof of the pub to collapse, killing seventeen people and injuring a further thirty. The bar was chosen as it was known to be popular with British soldiers, six of whom died in the attack.

1990

October – Patsy Gillespie, a Catholic cook working for the British Army, is taken from his home by masked IRA members. He is forced to drive a car filled with explosives to an army checkpoint on the Donegal border. The bomb is detonated by remote control, killing Gillespie and five British soldiers.

1993

March – Four Catholic men are shot dead by members of the UDA in Castlerock. Gerard Dalrymple (58), James McKenna (52) and Noel O'Kane (20) were civilians, while James Kelly (25) was an IRA volunteer.

October – The night before Halloween, members of the UFF open fire in the crowded Rising Sun pub in Greysteel. Eight people, Protestants and Catholics, are killed. One of the gunmen is said to have shouted 'trick or treat' before opening fire.

1994

Paramilitary groups on both sides agree to a ceasefire.

1995

October – Bellaghy-born poet Seamus Heaney receives the Nobel Prize for Literature.

	November – American President Bill Clinton visits Derry city.
1998	April – The Good Friday Agreement finally brings 'the Troubles' to an end.
	October – Derry's John Hume receives the Nobel Peace Prize, along with David Trimble.
2010	June – The Saville Report is published. It finds all the victims of Bloody Sunday innocent. British Prime Minister David Cameron apologises for the unjustifiable shootings.
2011	The Peace Bridge is opened.
2012	The Olympic Torch passes through Derry.
2013	Derry celebrates a year as the UK City of Culture.
2018	January – Sitcom *Derry Girls* premieres on Channel 4. By the end of the year the show and Derry-born writer Lisa McGee have won Radio Times and IFTA awards.

MOUNTSANDEL

It is believed that the first settlers to arrive in Ireland crossed the sea from Scotland. It is likely that this required boats, although it is not impossible that people could walk to Ireland from Britain at this time as fluctuating sea levels sometimes enabled land bridges to appear.

The earliest known settlement in Ireland is at Mountsandel, just outside Coleraine. It dates back to the Mesolithic age, which is roughly 8000-4500 BC.

The first settlers would have been hunter-gatherers who made use of the wide range of fish available from the River Bann and the surrounding forests, which were filled with fruit and nuts. The huts they lived in were made from saplings lashed together to form a sort of dome, similar in shape to an igloo, which would then be covered with animal skins or bark.

The site was excavated in the 1970s by Peter Woodman from University College Cork. During the excavation, many stone tools were found, including flint axes and needles. The team found the remains of seven buildings as well as charcoal used in cooking fires and evidence of other items used to prepare food. It is believed that this community would have been quite small, made up of perhaps just fifteen people at any one time.

Fragments of bones were also found at the site. It is likely that these bones are from wolves, given the time period, but they could possibly be dog bones, indicating one of the earliest examples of domesticated dogs in Europe.

MEGALITHIC TOMBS

Agriculture began in the Neolithic period in Ireland, as groups began to arrive from western Continental Europe with domesticated animals like cattle and pigs. Their way of life was more settled than that of people who lived at Mountsandel.

They would have preferred areas where they could grow crops and raise livestock and the resulting community became skilled in creating pottery and weapons.

This new settled community also buried their dead in elaborate stone tombs with weapons, food and other items from the person's life.

There are examples of these structures across Derry, like Ballybriest, or Carnanbane Court Tomb near Feeny is an example of a very large 'court' tomb, which is among the oldest types of tomb and is mainly found in the north of Ireland.

A good example of a 'wedge' tomb, one of the most common of such structures, is Well Glass Spring Tomb, near Limavady. The remains of six adults and two children were found when this tomb was excavated in the 1930s.

THE BROIGHTER HOARD

In 1896 two farm labourers stumbled upon some hard metal objects while ploughing a field at Broighter, near Limavady. They brought their findings to their employer and after the items were washed in the sink by a maid, it was clear that the find was very valuable. It has been suggested though, that the maid was not particularly careful washing the items and some gold pieces may have been washed down the drain!

The men had uncovered decorated gold items including jewellery, a bowl and a model boat complete with little oars. The owner of the farm sold the items to a Derry jeweller, where they were bought by Robert Day, a collector from Cork. He had the boat repaired, as it had been damaged by the plough and then he sold the lot to the British Museum for £600.

A dispute arose over who could rightfully claim ownership of the hoard. In 1903, this led to a court case in London. The case centred over the legal definitions of treasure. Treasure is defined as something which is voluntarily abandoned and if found is the property of those who found it. A trove, on the other hand, is something hidden with the intention of recovery at a later date or something lost accidentally. If a trove's rightful owner cannot be found, the Crown or State may claim the property.

The legal issue here was that the Royal Irish Academy (RIA), an academic body that aims to collect and preserve Irish archaeological artefacts, felt that the hoard should be removed from the British Museum and returned to Ireland. The museum argued that the hoard had been left voluntarily as an offering to the pagan sea god Manannán mac Lir and as a result was the property of those who found it, and then sold it to the museum.

Part of the case centred around the idea that the field at Broighter may have been underwater when the offering was made 2,000 years ago. The RIA asked naturalist Robert Lloyd Praeger, from County Down, to investigate this possibility. His team found an undisturbed Neolithic site near Portstewart and argued that as this site was older and undisturbed by the sea, then the Broighter field was also above sea level at the time and as a result a highly unlikely place to make an offering to a sea god.

The court ruled in the RIA's favour and declared that the find was a trove and was therefore the property of the State. The artefacts were given to the National Museum of Ireland, where they remain to this day. They were also loaned briefly for an exhibition in Limavady in November 2013.

MONASTIC DERRY

The *Annals of Ulster* record the founding of a monastery at Derry in 546 by St Columba, also called Colmcille. As a result, the settlement became an important centre for Christianity in Ireland and a community grew up around the holy men. By 720 Derry is known to have had a scriptorium, a room used for producing and copying elaborate manuscripts.

Monasteries at the time would also have housed crosses, chalices and other artefacts made from precious metals. This made these places very attractive for a Viking raid. The records show that the Irish defeated Vikings near Derry in the 830s and 860s yet continued to suffer through their raids into the late tenth century.

O'CAHAN COUNTRY

The O'Cahan clan are described as distant descendants of Niall of the Nine Hostages that established themselves between the Foyle and the Bann in the tenth and eleventh centuries. This area is named in the Annals as Ciannacht (or Keenaght), which encompasses the modern-day Roe Valley.

Their main stronghold was once on the banks of the Roe. The ruins can be seen today in the Roe Valley Country Park. Their overlords were the O'Neill clan of Tír Eoghain (modern-day Tyrone) and the O'Cahans, as their most powerful vassals, had the privilege of acting as 'kingmakers' for the O'Neills. The new O'Neill chief could only be inaugurated in a ceremony during which a member of the O'Cahan clan would throw a special brass shoe over his head.

They were constantly at war with neighbouring clans, particularly the O'Donnells in modern-day Donegal and the McQuillans of the coastal areas near Coleraine. However, they did not face real danger until the arrival of the Normans, particularly one John de Courcy. He arrived in Ireland in the 1170s and established a base in Coleraine. From there he attacked O'Cahan lands, burning many churches along the way. He was later challenged by the arrival of fellow Norman Hugh de Lacy. He was no saviour for the O'Cahans though, and led his own invasion of their lands, killing their chieftain on his way to confront de Courcy, whom he captured in 1203.

After this, the O'Cahans' power diminished greatly and their lands were controlled by various Normans. Their clan was hit particularly hard by the loss of fifteen of their chiefs in the battle of Drom Deirg, also known as the battle of Down. This battle saw Bryan O'Neill fail in his bid to become high king, as his Norman enemies had superior armour and weaponry.

Norman power eventually waned following the death of the 'Red' Earl of Ulster, Richard de Burgo in 1326. The O'Cahans sought to reassert themselves and build strongholds in Dungiven and on a crannog (an artificial island) in Enagh Lough. They again made war with neighbouring clans but on occasion fought outsiders. Sometimes mercenaries from Scotland known as 'gallowglasses' were hired to help them in battle. These soldiers are described as extremely fierce and could stand firm against Norman archers. They intermarried with the Irish, so it is likely there are a few people of gallowglass stock still living in the Roe Valley area.

Cumhaighe (Cooey) O'Cahan, whose name means 'Terror of the Stranger', was a chieftain of the clan in the last part of the fourteenth century. His exploits led to him being taken prisoner by the English in Coleraine and he was taken away, in chains, to Carrickfergus in 1376. Yet he was a well-respected chieftain and was buried in Dungiven upon his death in 1385. His tomb can still be seen today at the Augustinian priory in the town. His tomb is adorned with the figures of six gallow-glasses, who served as his bodyguards.

Several members of the clan died in strange circumstances over the years. Manus O'Cahan died after being wounded by a javelin in 1205. In January 1526, Geoffrey O'Cahan froze to death while on a 'predatory incursion', and Conor O'Kane was burned alive in the church of Dunboe just five years later.

Their name survives today in the surname of O'Kane, which is still common in the Roe Valley. Their warrior ways continue with Banagher boxer Eamonn O'Kane, who won a gold medal at the 2010 Commonwealth Games as an amateur. He turned professional in 2011 and had 17 fights before retiring in 2015 with a record of 14 wins, 2 defeats and 1 draw.

DOCWRA AND O'DOHERTY

Queen Elizabeth I of England had great concerns regarding Ireland. She feared that Ireland could be used as a base by her enemy – Catholic Spain. The Irish also had a history of rebellion, the Nine Years' War, also known as Tyrone's Rebellion, was just the latest example. It began in 1594 when Gaelic Lords, led by the Earl of Tyrone, Hugh O'Neill, and Hugh O'Donnell of Donegal, made an alliance in a bid to end English rule in Ireland. Several years into the conflict, Sir Henry Docwra arrived in Derry with a force of 4,000 men. His aim was to drive a wedge between O'Neill and O'Donnell by cutting off supply lines between their strongholds in Tyrone and Donegal.

Docwra occupied and fortified Derry. He is considered to be the second founder of Derry. His right-hand man was Cahir O'Doherty. Docwra had confirmed O'Doherty as the Lord of Inishowen when his father died. Cahir, aged thirteen, worked and fought beside Docwra from then on. He was knighted in 1602 for bravery in battle and Docwra himself said that the progress they had made against the Gaelic Lords would have been impossible without young O'Doherty.

In 1606, Docwra sold his position as Governor of Derry and left Ireland. The new governor, Sir George Paulett, had little respect for Catholics or the Irish and was soon eyeing up O'Doherty's estates in Inishowen. Following the 'Flight of the Earls' in 1607 – when O'Neill, O'Doherty and the Gaelic Lords gave up the ghost and fled to mainland Europe – Paulett attempted to seize one of O'Doherty's castles.

O'Doherty began to feel that he was under suspicion from the Crown. The king's deputy, Sir Arthur Chichester, demanded sureties from Cahir as proof of his loyalty. O'Doherty was deeply offended and refused to pay, which earned him the humiliation of a trip to the dungeon of Dublin Castle.

The final straw for O'Doherty came in April 1608. During an argument Paulett had arrogantly insisted that O'Doherty was not his equal and struck him. That same month O'Doherty rallied around 100 men, captured Derry and killed Paulett. There was some small resistance, but with little hope of reinforcements these men negotiated with O'Doherty and were allowed to leave, relatively unharmed. O'Doherty's men then ransacked the settlement and burnt it to the ground, leaving only 'chimneys and some stone walls standing'.

O'Doherty attempted to carry on his rebellion into Donegal but Chichester sent troops to face him. They laid siege to his castle at Burt and O'Doherty was killed, aged twenty-one, in July. His head was put on a spike in Dublin. The rebellion had lasted just eleven weeks.

PLANTATION AND REBELLION

After the Flight of the Earls and the O'Doherty uprising in 1608, the Crown decided that the best way to handle Ulster was to 'plant' the area with loyal Protestant settlers.

Members of London trade guilds were approached to take land in the new 'County Londonderry', London was added to the name Derry in honour of the guilds, which included the guilds of Vintners, Ironmongers, Goldsmiths and Clothworkers, among other trades.

'The Honourable The Irish Society' was created to oversee the plantation scheme and represent the guilds.

In 1613 the society was given 'The Charter of Londonderry,' a royal document marking the intention to build a new city. They built walls and defences around the city as part of the agreement, which were constructed between 1613 and 1619.

Towns and villages in County Derry were also established by the guilds. By 1610 'Newtownlimavady' was open for business as a town full of craftsmen and merchants. What would become Ballykelly grew from lands granted to the guild of Fishmongers in 1613, while Eglinton, then known as Muff, was founded in 1619 by the Grocer's company. The Skinner's company were granted lands in the areas around Dungiven, Claudy and Ballinascreen.

MASSACRE

When rebellion broke out in 1641, areas in Derry are initially quiet. However, by February 1642 fires could be seen across the country-side from Limavady to Eglinton. People sought shelter in Coleraine, Limavady and Derry city. Supplies quickly ran low in these settlements, and soldiers were attacked while trying to replenish their stores.

Troops from Donegal arrived under the command of Sir Robert Stewart. They spent a night in Derry and then set out for Coleraine. They ran into rebels between Limavady and Dungiven and, although outnumbered, Stewart forced the rebels to retreat.

Estimates vary wildly on the number of Protestants killed in the rebellion. Some accounts say 100,000 but somewhere closer to 4,000 is deemed to be more realistic by many historians. Regardless of the numbers, the massacres were undoubtedly brutal, yet not as extreme as English propaganda suggested at the time. These anti-Irish and anti-Catholic publications gave Oliver Cromwell 'justification' to bring his wrath down on Ulster and Ireland in 1649.

Cromwell committed atrocities of his own across Ireland, particularly in Drogheda and Wexford. Many suffered in County Derry during his campaign as settlers clashed with natives, hunger and disease ran rampant and Limavady was burned to the ground.

Derry city came under siege for the first time in May 1649 when a Presbyterian army tried to take the city from its Parliamentarian garrison. Sir Charles Coote, in command of the garrison, ordered the destruction of houses near to the walls to remove any possible cover for the attackers. It was August when the siege was finally broken, by a Catholic Irish army led by Eoghan Roe O'Neill.

As many as 616,000 Irish people are believed to have died as a result of Cromwell's campaign. Many of Cromwell's 35,000 soldiers were given land in Ireland in lieu of payment. Protestant settlers already living in Ireland also use the opportunity to expand their lands at the expense of Catholics.

When Charles II becomes king in 1660, he announces that soldiers can keep land gained during the conflict, except that belonging to Catholics who had not been involved. This does little to improve the anti-Catholic feeling in England and neither does the coronation of Charles's successor, the Catholic King James II.

When an heir is born to James, his opponents fear that an on-going Catholic monarchy is beginning. They approach James's Protestant sister Mary and her husband William of Orange and encourage them to take the throne. This marks the beginning of the Williamite Wars. When England quickly unites behind William, James plans to flee to France but decides instead to make Ireland his base.

SIEGE

The famous second siege of Derry lasted 105 days, from April to July 1689.

James's supporters in Ireland, the Jacobites, sought to secure important settlements in anticipation of his arrival but in December 1688, thirteen apprentice boys closed the gates of the city to prevent the Jacobite Earl of Antrim from entering and claiming the city.

James wanted to secure important ports like Derry, so after landing at Kinsale in March 1689, he quickly travelled north, gathering troops along the way and arrived at the city in April. The city's defenders fired at his army upon his arrival, an action that those in command of the city later apologised for in a formal letter to the king.

The Governor of Derry, Robert Lundy, had made great efforts to improve the city's walls and defences. Yet he lost heart in April 1689 and made plans to surrender the city to the Jacobites. However, by the time James arrived he had lost control of the city and the cries of 'No Surrender' from the walls ended any chance of negotiation. James left the siege to his general and departed just two days after his arrival.

The Jacobites caused devastation throughout the siege with cannon and mortars, which weighed around 120kg. They also built a boom across the Foyle, in an attempt to stop aid being brought to the city by sea.

Protestant civilians had flocked to the city when the gates had been open, although many were forced to camp outside the walls. Their presence put added strain on the city's already limited resources. Lack of food and poor sanitation in the city meant conditions were ideal for the spread of fever and disease.

As the siege wore on, the defenders were forced to eat horses and dogs. In an act of desperation the last cow left in the city was tied to a stake outside the walls and set alight. The plan was that its cries would attract nearby cows belonging to the enemy, but had the opposite effect of scaring them away. A fat gentleman also thought it wise to hide himself away from public areas and the greedy eye of some soldiers.

Yet the defenders would not relent and on 28 July the Jacobite boom was broken by the *Mountjoy*, a Williamite ship, and the city was relieved.

Estimates suggest that less than half of the people in the city when the gates were shut to Jacobite forces in December 1688 lived to see its relief in July 1689.

Today the Siege of Derry is commemorated by the Apprentice Boys each year. In December they remember the 'shutting of the gates' and celebrate the relief of the city in August. Artefacts from the siege can be seen in the city's museums, St Columb's Cathedral and the Apprentice Boys' Memorial Hall.

In 1690 the armies of William and James met on the banks of the river Boyne. James had 25,000 troops, while William has 36,000. Some 2,000 die in the ensuing battle, mostly Jacobites, and William was victorious. James retreated, causing many more of his troops to desert him, while William marched on to secure Dublin. The Battle of Aughrim in July 1691 brought an end to the remaining Jacobite forces in Ireland.

William's victory is widely celebrated on the 'Glorious Twelfth', particularly by the Orange Order who parade across Northern Ireland. Part of these celebrations focus on Lundy, who had attempted to surrender the city. A giant effigy of the famous 'traitor' is burned each year, although it is likely that the improvements he made to the city's defences enabled the defenders to hold out.

FAMINE AND EMIGRATION

The population of Ireland grew significantly in the eighteenth century. Many people were dependant on the potato, as the crop can grow in poor land and produces a high yield. The potato crops failed in 1739 and again in 1740, leading to starvation and the death of nearly a quarter of the population.

This was just the beginning of the problem as poor agricultural techniques and over-farming took its toll on the land. The potato crop failed again in 1800, between 1816 and 1819 and in 1822.

These crop failures were overshadowed when the 'Great Hunger' began in 1845. A fungal disease took hold of the potato crop, causing them to rot in the ground. Hunger and contagious diseases like cholera ravaged the country. The famine claimed the lives of around a million people across Ireland. Figures from the 1851 census indicate that 25,883 people died in County Derry during the famine.

Two million people also emigrated, mainly to Britain, Australia and America. The port of Derry was the last sight that many Irish emigrants saw before their journey to the United States and Canada. They travelled in awful conditions on 'coffin ships' which were over-crowded and riddled with disease. Many died during their voyage.

One such ship was called *Londonderry*. It left Sligo bound for Liverpool, but was forced to take shelter from a storm in Derry. The ship's crew had forced steerage passengers into the hold when the storm began and when the ship docked it was found that many had died of suffocation. Of those who died, seventy-two were men, while women and children were 'piled four deep'.

The *Exmouth* also sailed from Derry in 1847. Built to carry around 170 passengers, it set sail for Quebec carrying 203 adults, sixty-three children and nine infants. It was wrecked on an island off the coast of Scotland and only three people survived.

INDUSTRY

The production of shirts would become a defining industry in Derry city. In 1831 William Scott set up the first shirt business, which employed 'out-workers' from the countryside who would collect materials from nearby stations, make the shirts and then return the completed articles to the stations, which were scattered around the north west.

This practice would change in the 1850s with the invention of the sewing machine. William Tillie, a shirt manufacturer from Glasgow, was one of the first to set up a factory with his partner John Henderson. The factory was the largest in the world at the time and was famous enough to be mentioned by Karl Marx in his book *Das Kapital*.

The shirt industry meant that a large number of women were employed in Derry compared to other areas. In 1902, 80 per cent of workers in Derry's shirt industry were female and by the 1920s there were forty-four factories in the city with 18,000 employees.

The industry declined after the Second World War, when clothing from developing countries began to flood into the British market. The last of the traditional shirt factories, Glenaden Shirts in the Waterside, closed in 2008.

THE FIRST WORLD WAR

Men from both sides of the community in Derry went to Europe to fight in the First World War. Perhaps the best example of the sacrifice that people from the area made at this time is that of the Stewart brothers from Dungiven, William, George, Hugh and Isaac.

George Stewart had emigrated to Canada. When the war began he was sent to France as part of the Canadian Expeditionary Force. He died, aged twenty-eight, on Tor Top Ridge in June 1916.

A few weeks later his brother Isaac went into action and fought on the Somme. He survived the war and lived until 1968. His brother Hugh also survived the war. Hugh enlisted in 1915 and fought on the Somme for two months before being injured and evacuated.

William, the eldest brother, served with the Australian Army. He fought in Egypt, Gallipoli and on the Somme. He was killed instantly by a shell, four days before the Battle of the Somme came to an end. He was only 30 years old.

Their sister was also involved in the war effort. Margaret Alice Stewart worked in the coding section of the Women's Royal Naval Service until 1919.

Two stained-glass windows were installed in Dungiven Presbyterian Church to commemorate those who had served in the First World War. Margaret was invited to unveil one of the brass plaques listing the dead, including her two dead brothers.

War memorials were erected to commemorate the dead across the county. The Derry City Memorial was designed by sculptor Vernon March and erected in 1927.

PARTITION OF IRELAND

Following the Easter Rising in 1916, the few potential troublemakers in Derry were rounded up and interned. The city remained calm, mainly because so many fighting men were at war in Europe.

However, sectarian violence erupted in the city when the First World War ended in 1918 and the Irish War of Independence began in 1919. As the partition of Ireland grew close, riots broke out in 1920, resulting in the deaths of forty people. Several members of the IRA were interned and executed in Derry Gaol during the conflict. Derry became a border city and county in 1921, when Ireland was partitioned.

THE SECOND WORLD WAR

As in the First World War, thousands of Derry natives signed up to fight in Europe between 1939 and 1945. However, the city itself would play a key role in the conflict.

Close to 40,000 Allied military personnel came to Derry during the war, nearly doubling the population of the city. As a result, numerous military facilities like airfields, barracks and listening posts were built across the county.

The most important constructions were two naval bases. Early in the war the British Navy took over Ebrington Barracks and named it

HMS *Ferret*. American personnel also worked there before a US Naval base, the first of its kind in Europe, was constructed nearby in 1942. The bases provided vital support to the Allies during the Battle of the Atlantic as the United Kingdom's most westerly port. As well as having an important base for repairing and refuelling ships, crews came to Derry to be trained in anti-submarine warfare.

Yet the prominence of this base made Derry a target. In April 1941, a German plane dropped two bombs on the city. One landed in Messines Park, killing thirteen people. The other landed near a church and did relatively little damage. A witness said that the church was about to be directly hit by the bomb when a statue of St Patrick just outside of the building shoved the bomb out of the way at the last minute.

At the end of the war, more than sixty Nazi U-boats came to Derry to surrender. Many of these were later towed out to sea near the city and sunk.

During the war, the Derry area was not only of strategic importance but was also favoured by many servicemen due to its proximity to the border with the neutral Irish Free State. This meant that luxuries like meat and butter could be enjoyed in much larger quantities than the rations available in the United Kingdom.

UNDER SUSPICION

Victor Fiorentini, an Italian businessman, had set up a restaurant in Derry city after the First World War. Following Mussolini's rise to power in Italy, Fiorentini helped to establish a Derry branch of the Fascist Party, which brought him to the attention of the local authorities.

In 1939, he was warned that if Italy joined the war in support of the Nazis that he would be interned. Mussolini did come to Hitler's support in June 1940 and Fiorentini managed to escape the police just in time by taking a car just across the border to Muff, in County Donegal. After three years he managed to convince the authorities that he was not passing information to the Axis powers and was allowed to return to Derry, his business and his wife.

THE TROUBLES

The Northern Ireland Civil Rights Association (NICRA) was formed in 1967. The organisation demanded equal rights for Catholics from a State that they felt only served the interest of Protestants. They organised public marches to put pressure on the government. However, these protests were often met with a violent response from Loyalists. For example, a march from Belfast to Derry in January 1969 was ambushed at Burntollet Bridge. Three hundred marchers were injured and it is claimed that the police did little to protect them. Rioting broke out in Derry and became common in the months that followed. After an intense riot at an Apprentice Boys parade in August 1969, British soldiers were sent to Northern Ireland in an attempt to contain the situation.

The troops were initially welcomed by Nationalists as a possible alternative to the Royal Ulster Constabulary (RUC), a police force they no longer trusted. Yet by 1970 they were seen as another instrument of Unionist rule. Paramilitary groups were formed around this time. The Provisional IRA saw themselves as defenders of the Catholic community, while the Ulster Volunteer Force (UVF) and the Ulster Defence Association (UDA) wanted to preserve the Union from the threat of the growing political voice of Catholics.

The introduction of internment – imprisonment without trial – further soured relationships between Nationalists and the British Army. This move only increased rioting and swelled the ranks of paramilitary groups.

In January 1972 a march, policed by British soldiers, was arranged to take place in Derry to protest against internment. During this march, members of the Parachute Regiment opened fire on the crowd. They fired 108 rounds, killing thirteen protesters and injuring many more. The soldiers claimed that they had come under fire from the crowd. An investigation later in the year produced the Widgery Report, which exonerated the British Army and blamed the tragedy on NICRA for having organised an 'illegal march'. Lord Chief Justice Widgery accepted the many of the victims had been unarmed, but also accepted the claims of soldiers that they had been fired upon first.

The report deeply angered the Nationalist community who felt it was a 'whitewash'. After a lengthy campaign for another inquiry, Lord Saville was appointed in 1998 to investigate the events of Bloody Sunday. The Saville Report, published in June 2010, stated that the soldiers fired the first shot and none of the marchers that were killed or injured had posed a threat to the troops. The British Prime Minister David Cameron made an apology for the 'unjustified and unjustifiable' events of Bloody Sunday. The families of victims welcomed the report and the long-awaited vindication of their relatives.

Following Bloody Sunday, the Nationalist community was dismayed at the political situation in Northern Ireland. Although they continued to support groups advocating peaceful means of achieving rights for Catholics, like the Social Democratic and Labour Party (SDLP), the violence meant that more people turned to the Provisional IRA. Violence would continue throughout Northern Ireland in the 1970s and 1980s as British forces and Loyalist paramilitaries clashed with the IRA.

In 1981, republican prisoners went on hunger strike in a bid to be recognised as political prisoners. Ten hunger strikers starved themselves to death, several of whom were from Derry city, Bellaghy and Dungiven. During this time the Provisional IRA conducted a bombing campaign in Britain. Notable attacks included an attack on Harrod's department store in London, the murder of Earl Mountbatten in County Sligo and an attempt on Prime Minister Margaret Thatcher's life during the 1984 Conservative Party Conference in Brighton.

MODERN DERRY

Talks between SDLP leader John Hume and Gerry Adams of Sinn Féin paved the way for a peaceful resolution to the Troubles. In 1994, paramilitaries from both sides announced ceasefires. The Peace Process slowly moved forward as representatives from the Irish, British and American governments became involved in the negotiations. American President Bill Clinton spoke in Derry city in November 1995, urging both sides to reach an agreement.

Following extensive talks in 1998, it was announced on Good Friday that an agreement had been reached. The Good Friday Agreement would go on to form the basis of Northern Ireland's future government.

Derry, both as a city and a county, has progressed in leaps and bounds after leaving behind the dark days of the Troubles. The city, once the scene of violent riots and no-go areas, is now an attractive venue for major events like the Turner Prize, the Clipper Round the World Yacht Race and concerts organised by the BBC and MTV.

The most visible symbol of the city's bright future is perhaps the Peace Bridge, built in 2011. The footbridge physically overcomes the divide between the largely Unionist Waterside and the largely Nationalist Cityside. It also allows access to Ebrington Square, a shared space for the city's residents, on the site of what was once a British Army base.

2

PEOPLE

Derry is a place that punches above its weight. The area can boast many natives, as well as those with roots in the Oak Leaf county, that have performed well on the world stage, including world leaders and Nobel Prize winners.

Others have become famous only locally, from revolutionaries and inventors to 'buck eejits', as Derry folk would say.

NATIVES

Jimmy Allender (1848-1886)

The man who would become Derry's gentle giant began in humble circumstances. His father died while he was young and his mother was forced to place him in an orphanage.

In his twenties, he was said to be seven and half, or even eight, feet tall. He began to appear in exhibitions as a giant around this time. There is a tale of him performing on stage with the world's smallest man, Charles Stratton. Stratton was barely three feet high and performed under the name 'General' Tom Thumb. The idea was that the two would re-enact scenes from *Gulliver's Travels*, with Thumb and his fellow 'little people' portraying the residents of Lilliput.

Allender left Derry in 1876, bound for Philadelphia. The story goes that he met the famous P.T. Barnum in the United States. Another rumour states that he worked in the very Philadelphia tavern in which Thomas Jefferson had written the Declaration of Independence 100 years before.

After little success in America and on tours of mainland Europe, Allender is believed to have toured England with a Derry lady known as 'the Fattest Woman'. He died following a short illness in South Shields, where he was buried.

He left instructions that he was to be buried beneath twelve feet of solid rock, to deter 'scientists' eager to dissect his body. Despite this his remains were exhumed in 1972 and presented to the world.

Alexander Anderson (1858-1936)

Born in Coleraine, Anderson was a pioneering physicist in many fields. He was educated at Queen's College Galway and then Cambridge. He became Professor of Natural Philosophy on his return to Galway, a post he held for nearly fifty years.

The theory in electrical engineering, Anderson's Bridge, is named for him. He is now perhaps best known as the first physicist to consider what might happen if a star collapsed under its own gravity – a theory which suggests the existence of black holes.

Gerry Anderson (1944-2014)

For thirty years Gerry Anderson was a much-loved voice on BBC Radio Foyle. His irreverent show provided locals with endless entertainment and he made one of the more sensible contributions to the Derry or Londonderry name debate. Anderson elected to call it 'Stroke City'. He died following a long illness on 21 August 2014.

William Beatty (1773-1842)

William Beatty came from a prominent family in Derry city. His great-grandfather was Captain Beatty, one of the city's defenders against James II.

He joined the navy and quickly found himself following in the footsteps of fellow Ulstermen George Magrath and Leonard Gillespie into the service of Admiral Nelson.

He was the surgeon aboard the HMS *Victory* during the Battle of Trafalgar. He had to perform ten amputations during the battle and reported cases of gangrene among the wounded sailors. He also tended to Admiral Nelson when he was shot. As he felt Nelson was beyond treatment, Beatty could offer him little more than comfort in his final moments.

His account of Nelson's death was popular, although the title was rather long-winded, *Authentic Narrative of the Death of Lord Nelson, with the Circumstances Preceding, Attending and Subsequent to that Event, the Professional Report of His Lordship's Wound and Several Interesting Anecdotes*. It contained the famous last words of the admiral to his friend – 'Kiss me, Hardy.' However, some claim he really said '*Kismet*, Hardy', *kismet* being a Turkish word for destiny.

Charles Byrne (1761-83)

Byrne is believed to have been born in Drummullan, near the border between Derry and Tyrone. For this reason he is identified as a Derry or Tyrone man by different sources. He stood a little over seven feet seven inches tall and found fame in his twenties by exhibiting himself as a 'freak' in London.

He drank heavily and died aged just twenty-two. Surgeon John Hunter, who acquired the body by bribing (some say tricking) Byrne's friends, boiled the body down to its skeleton and placed it in the Hunterian Museum, part of the Royal College of Surgeons in London. His skeleton has remained there on display for over 230 years.

However, according to the *British Medical Journal*, becoming one of Hunter's exhibits was one of Byrne's worst nightmares.

Before his death, he had expressed a wish to be buried at sea. In 2011 several academics, including Queen's University lawyer Thomas Muinzer, appealed to the museum to respect Byrne's wishes and bury the body at sea. The museum rejected this appeal and the skeleton remains on display today.

Despite his impressive height, at the time Byrne was not even the tallest person in Ireland. That title goes to Cork man Patrick Cotter O'Brien, also known as the 'Irish Giant', He stood approximately eight feet one inch, which was verified when his remains were exhumed in 1972. Byrne is also believed to have been related to the tallest twins in history, the Knipe Brothers of Magherafelt, who were seven feet two inches tall.

Byrne has been immortalised in fiction by Hilary Mantel in her 1998 novel *The Giant, O'Brien*. He was also mentioned in passing by Charles Dickens in *David Copperfield*.

In addition to this, research has found that Byrne's height was the result of a rare gene mutation called familial isolated pituitary adenoma, which was discovered in 2006. Six-foot-nine Tyrone man Brendan Holland was also found to have the mutation and after some analysis it was discovered that Holland was related to Byrne.

James Campbell (1826-1900)

Campbell, the eighth child of twelve siblings, was born in Derry city. At 13 years old he was a stowaway on a boat bound for Canada and soon found his way to his brother's home in New York.

At the age of 15 he joined a whaling crew sailing around the Pacific Horn. When the ship was wrecked, Campbell managed to float to an island on a piece of debris. His relief was short-lived though, as he was captured by the island's natives. A source states that these people were cannibals who tied Campbell to a tree while they discussed his fate. Campbell managed to ingratiate himself with the tribe's chief by repairing a musket and eventually he managed to escape to Tahiti.

He settled in Hawaii and built up an empire by setting up a sugar processing company. He quickly became extremely wealthy as a result of clever investments in land that was thought to be arid and worthless. In 2006 his fortune was estimated to be worth around $2.3 billion in today's money.

He found himself in captivity again in 1896 when he was kidnapped by a man called Oliver Winthrop. After being lured to a house in San Francisco, a masked man put a gun to Campbell's head and told him to raise his hands. Then aged seventy, he is reported to have replied, 'I'll be damned if I throw up my hands! Go ahead and shoot me!' before lunging for the gun and wrestling his attacker. The gun went off during the struggle, grazing Campbell's temple and putting a hole through his hat. Winthrop then knocked him out.

Over the next few days, Campbell was chained to a bed, beaten and threatened as his captors attempted to get him to sign a cheque for $20,000. Campbell refused and endured this ordeal despite two days without food or water. Eventually, the men gave up and let Campbell go, even going as far as to give him money for transport and a new hat.

Campbell returned to his hotel and spoke to the authorities. After a brief court case, Winthrop was sentenced to life imprisonment in San Quentin and is believed to have died around 1910.

Thomas Gallaher (1840-1927)

Gallaher, originally from Templemoyle, started out as an apprentice in a company that imported tobacco and tea. Within two years, he had picked up the basics and set up his own business, aged just seventeen, rolling and selling tobacco from a cart.

He moved to Belfast and set up shop in 1863, still in his early twenties. Before long, he was making regular trips to America to buy his own tobacco leaf. In 1896, Gallaher expanded his business and opened what was then the biggest tobacco factory in the world in Belfast.

His business, the Gallaher Group, became one of the world's largest tobacco companies, buying over big brands like Benson & Hedges and Liggett Ducat, the number one brand in Russia. In 2006 the Gallaher Group was bought by Japan Tobacco in a £7.5 billon deal.

Thomas Gallaher is described as having been a good employer, with sympathy for migrants from rural areas like himself. He introduced paid holidays and reduced his employees' working hours. One employee recalls that in his old age Gallaher would fill his pockets with twists of tobacco and hand them out to the unemployed men that gathered outside the factory.

Henry Haslett (1758-1806)

Born in Limavady, Haslett made his way to Belfast and became involved in shipping and insurance. He was one of the founding members of the United Irish Society in 1791, along with Theobald Wolfe Tone and Henry Joy McCracken.

He and seven other United Irishmen were arrested in 1796 on charges of high treason. During the fourteen months he spent in Kilmainham Jail two of his children and his sister died. He is buried in Belfast's Knockbreda Cemetery.

Frederick Hervey (1730-1803)

The 'Earl Bishop' was born the Fourth Earl of Bristol and entered the Church at the age of 24. He became Bishop of Derry and Raphoe in 1768. He seems to have had little time for cronyism and is said to have made portly priests who were eager to further their positions strip down and compete in midnight runs through bogs.

He was in favour of liberal reform as evidenced by his support of Catholic Emancipation and the fact he donated money and stone for the construction of the Catholic Long Tower church.

He made important contributions to both Derry city and county. In the city, he championed the construction of the first bridge across the Foyle. Although it was relatively simple, the fact that people no longer had to rely on ferryboats to cross the river revolutionised travel and industry. He also built impressive residences at Downhill and Ballyscullion.

John Hume (1937-)

Hume is one of Derry city's best-known natives. In his youth he was an altar boy and paper boy who was on course for the priesthood. He attended the seminary in Maynooth, County Kildare, after leaving St Columb's College, but dropped out after three years to become a secondary school teacher.

He became involved with the local community by helping to set up a credit union and by campaigning for a proposed university to be built in Derry. He also somehow found time to run a small smoked salmon business.

A decision was made to build the New University of Ulster in Coleraine, an overwhelmingly unionist town. The move has been described by Hume as being the 'spark that ignited the civil rights movement' and he has said that the choice meant that any 'chance of orderly change in Northern Ireland probably disappeared'.

Following this, Hume quickly became a leading figure in the civil rights movement with the Derry Citizen's Action Committee (DCAC). He was also a founding member of the SDLP and became its leader in 1979. With the party he served as a politician in the Northern Ireland Assembly and represented the Foyle constituency in Westminster. He also served as a Member of the European Parliament for over twenty years from 1979 until 2004.

Hume is regarded as one of the greatest politicians to come from Northern Ireland. He fostered strong relationships with American leaders and conducted negotiations with Sinn Féin leader Gerry Adams. As a result, he was instrumental in bringing about the Good Friday Agreement.

He received the Nobel Peace Prize with the Ulster Unionist Party's David Trimble in 1998. He has also been the recipient of the Gandhi Peace Prize and the Martin Luther King Award. He was the first person to be awarded all three of the major peace awards.

He stepped down as leader of the SDLP and retired from politics in 2004.

In 2010, he was voted as 'Ireland's Greatest' by RTÉ viewers in Ireland, beating figures like James Joyce, Brian O'Driscoll and Phil Lynott to take the title.

William Massey (1856-1925)

William Ferguson Massey was born into a farming family in Limavady. He completed his education in the town before moving to New Zealand in 1870.

He became involved in politics through his work with the local community and was particularly concerned with agricultural issues. He became a member of parliament in 1894 and served the rural Franklin area from 1896 until his death.

He founded the Reform Party in 1909, which achieved great success in the 1911 election. The party failed to gain an absolute majority, yet the following year the ruling Labour Party lost a vote of confidence and could no longer stay in power.

In 1912 Massey became the nineteenth Prime Minister of New Zealand. He would remain in the role until his death thirteen years later, making him the second longest-serving New Zealand Prime Minister.

He led the country in incredibly difficult times. He visited New Zealand's injured First World War troops, including his own son and watched as an epidemic of influenza killed over 8,500 people when the war ended.

Massey University, which has campuses in Palmerston North, Wellington and Auckland, is named after him. Massey Avenue in Limavady is also named after him and a bronze statue of him can be seen outside the library on Irish Green Street.

Hudy McGuigan

Folk hero Hudy McGuigan lived in Ballinascreen during the nineteenth century. If we were feeling unkind he might be referred to as a village idiot, but otherwise entertainer or sportsman will suffice. There are a number of stories about his (usually naked) antics, which include riding around naked on his horse and leaping, naked again, over the pavilion of a local lord.

The most famous story about Hudy though concerns the two halves of a stable or horse door, that is the doors usually found in farms where the top half can be opened independently of the bottom. The story goes that Hudy was in the farmyard and witnessed a rooster fly a short distance. He figured that if a rooster could manage to fly a few yards then so could he.

So, he strapped half of a door to each arm and headed for a nearby cliff. He jumped off and after flapping the doors a bit came crashing to earth in a thorny bush. He survived his 'flight' with just a few broken bones.

In some versions of the tale he added feathers to the doors in the hope of improving the design of his makeshift 'wings', or made them entirely out of feathers.

From this adventure comes the nickname 'half-door' for some McGuigans, while Hudy himself is sometimes referred to as a 'quarter-clift', which means that he is not completely there mentally. The story is not as well known in Ireland as it once was (it may have influenced the decision to name Joyce's hero Stephen Dedalus) but he is remembered by a small path in the Sperrin Mountains that carries the name of the story's hero – Hudy's Way.

John Mitchel (1815-1875)

Mitchel was born in Camnish near Dungiven, but the family moved to Derry when he just four and then to Newry when he was eight. He began working as a solicitor in 1836 and it was in this role that Mitchel first became disturbed by the rate and volume of evictions across Ireland. He spoke of the injustice of 'whole neighbourhoods being thrown out upon the highways in winter'.

He became involved in political protests and contributed to *The Nation*, the paper of the Young Ireland movement. He would later set up his own popular paper, *The United Irishman*.

His sense of injustice intensified during the famine years of the mid-nineteenth century, which is seen in his writing that calls for the starving people to revolt. He was arrested in 1848, tried by jury and sentenced to fourteen years 'transportation for treason'. He would reach Van Diemen's Land in Tasmania, Australia, two years after his sentence, during which time he wrote *My Jail Journal*.

He managed to escape to New York in 1853, where he again took up journalism, setting up *The Citizen*. He found himself behind bars again in America, this time for articles justifying slavery, by claiming that slaves led better lives than many of the Irish. He eventually returned to Ireland and is buried in Newry.

John Mitchel Place in Newry bears his name today, as does Dungiven's Mitchel Park and John Mitchel's GAC in Claudy.

John Edward McCullough (1832-1885)

When his mother died, 15-year-old McCullough was sent away from Coleraine to live with relatives in Philadelphia. He became a popular Shakespearian actor and earned particular praise for his portrayal of Othello.

He shared the stage with Edwin Booth, who saved Abraham Lincoln's son from being hit by a train. Edwin's brother, John Wilkes Booth, was also an actor and appeared in a play for the benefit of McCullough in March 1864 at Ford's Theatre, Washington DC. Less than a month later, John Wilkes Booth assassinated President Lincoln in the very same theatre.

McCullough is said to have been a close friend of the assassin and apparently fled to Canada following the president's death to avoid being questioned by the authorities. Some believe that he would have known enough about Booth's intentions to have saved Lincoln's life and could have received a prison sentence for his inaction.

Another story goes that he got into an argument with a fellow actor, either over the affections of an actress, or the privilege of playing a prominent role. The other actor is said to have shot and killed McCullough backstage in 1885 and got rid of the body by burying it under the stage at the National Theatre in Washington.

His ghost is said to haunt the theatre but he is rumoured to be more helpful than scary, as he is often seen checking props and making sure the theatre is ready for the next performance. There are supposedly sightings of him all around the theatre, in dressing rooms, on the stage and as part of the audience.

However, the story of his shooting seems to be entirely fictional. He stopped acting when he was diagnosed with general paresis, a disorder of the brain caused by syphilis. He spent a year in an insane asylum, before his death in 1885.

It became popular to go to watch his 'insane ramblings', while he was in the asylum. His ravings would be imitated in one of the earliest audio recordings in history, possibly with the involvement of Thomas Edison. These recordings can still be found online today.

Charles 'Nomad' McGuinness (1893-1947)

Aged just fifteen, McGuinness ran away from his childhood home in Derry city to pursue a life of adventure on the seas. By the time he was 16, he had already sailed around the world, visiting Chile, New York, Australia and Tahiti.

From there, his stories – taken from his own accounts – get a bit far-fetched. Before he returned to Derry in 1914, he is said to have been shipwrecked, taken part in mutinies on ships, mined for gold in Australia, was homeless in Canada and spent time in a dungeon in Venice.

He joined the British military, probably the navy, at the start of the Second World War and saw action in Africa, before deserting the army and fighting on the German side. He made a trip to Asia in 1919 where he was a pirate and the lover of an 'oriental princess'.

Back in Derry in 1921, he was an assassin and bank robber working with the IRA. He was caught and jailed in Ebrington Barracks until he escaped using either the classic file smuggled in a cake trick, or by being smuggled out in a coffin. After a brief trip south to become the first Irishman to visit the South Pole, he went to America, where he received the US Congressional Gold Medal for Antarctic exploration as part of Rear Admiral Byrd's first Antarctic expedition and also worked as a bootlegger.

He spent time in Russia in the 1930s and was in Spain during the civil war. He again returned to Ireland, wrote some articles for the *Irish Independent* and had confrontations with Nazi spies.

The official story goes that McGuinness died in a shipwreck off Wexford in 1947, but some suspect he really faked his death to travel to the Pacific in secret. In his life he had claimed to know where a mysterious hoard of pirate treasure, the 'Treasure of Lima' was located. Some think that he survived the shipwreck and went to claim this treasure for himself.

The treasure is said to have included over 1,000 diamonds, 200 chests of jewels, and various golden statues, crowns and chalices. It is rumoured to be worth nearly £150 million today. The treasure has been hunted by many explorers since, including Franklin D. Roosevelt and actor Errol Flynn.

Sir James Murray (1788-1871)

Born in Culnady, near Maghera, Murray was educated in Edinburgh and Dublin before setting himself up as a surgeon and apothecary in Belfast in 1808.

When the Marquis of Anglesey, then Lord Lieutenant of Ireland, complained of stomach pain, Murray designed a 'fluid magnesia' to treat him. This product was patented two years after his death and is sold worldwide today as Milk of Magnesia.

Murray also experimented with the creation and use of artificial fertilisers and is considered to be a pioneer in the field. He is commemorated by a blue plaque at 16 High Street Belfast, which was his former home.

Oliver Pollock (1737-1823)

Originally from Coleraine, Pollack emigrated first to Philadelphia and later to Havana, Cuba. He was an extremely successful merchant by the time he made his way to New Orleans in 1767.

He is credited with inventing the US dollar sign ($) in 1788. Although some believe the symbol derives from placing a U over an S (as in United States), it appears it comes from placing an S over a P – as in Spanish peso, the model for the US dollar.

Charles Tegart (1881-1946)

Following his education at Portora Royal School in Enniskillen and Trinity College Dublin, Tegart, a native of Derry city, moved to India in 1901.

He served with the Calcutta Police as a detective for thirty years, undertaking work that was extremely dangerous. A businessman who resembled Tegart was shot dead after being mistaken for the detective. Even though he was subjected to several assassination attempts, Tegart was undeterred and continued to drive in a car with an open top and his dog riding on the bonnet.

In 1936, he was sent to Palestine where the Arab population were in revolt, partly in protest against the rising Jewish population who had migrated to the country. He created a line of sixty-nine fortresses – known as Tegart forts – to prevent weapons being smuggled into the country from Lebanon and Syria.

He used extreme methods to interrogate insurgents. The Arab Investigation Centres set up under his direction were places that saw Palestinians tortured with extremely cruel measures like waterboarding, being left in open cages in the sun and having red hot skewers and boiling oil used on their bodies.

He was a tough man in an extremely tough job. He kept a defused bomb on his desk to use as a paperweight. Yet one day, he threw this paperweight in anger only for it to explode against the wall. Tegart reportedly laughed the incident off.

Charles Thomson (1729-1824)

Thomson was born in Gorteade, near Maghera. His mother died when he was young and soon after Thomson, then 10, emigrated to America with his father and siblings. His father died on the journey, allegedly when in sight of land. The children were raised in Delaware by a blacksmith. Thomson went on to become a Latin tutor at the Philadelphia Academy.

In 1774 he became Secretary of the American Continental Congress, the governing body of the United States during the Revolution. He held the post for fifteen years. This role would lead some to later call him the 'Prime Minister of the United States'. He was described as reliable and well-rounded in his work, but this did not prevent him from rising to a challenge from James Searle in Congress. Searle said he had been misquoted by Thomson and the two had a cane fight in the chamber, which ended with them both being slashed across the face.

On 4 July 1776, he was one of only two people, along with John Hancock, to sign the first published version of the Declaration of Independence. Hancock then sent the document to printer John Dunlap, himself a Strabane native, to have copies made. The original document has been lost, but some copies remain. These 'Dunlap Broadsides' were sent across the country to rally the people to the American cause.

In August, the famous Declaration of Independence was signed, but for some reason Thomson was not included this time. However, he is remembered in the United States for having designed the Great American Seal, which appears on the one-dollar bill and on which the Presidential Seal is based.

When George Washington was elected as the country's first president, it was Thomson who was sent to Virginia to give him the news.

VISITORS

Dr Raphael Ernest Grail Armattoe (1913-1953)

'The Irishman from West Africa,' as Armattoe was named by the *New York Post*, was born in the German colony of Togoland. The area was divided up after the Second World War, meaning young Raphael learned English, French and German from a young age.

He left Africa at the age of 17 and was educated in Germany and France before qualifying to practise medicine in Edinburgh. He then moved to Derry, set up a medical practice and worked there throughout the war. Those who remember him said that he turned heads as one of the very few black people in the city at the time.

He gave lectures in the city on a variety of subjects, including anthropology. He also advocated the independence of African colonies on the world stage, speaking at the 1945 Pan-African Congress and the Scientific and Cultural Conference for World Peace in New York.

One of his stories caused quite a stir when it appeared on the front page of the *Londonderry Sentinel* in January 1946. In it he claimed to know that the Soviet Union had surpassed the Americans in nuclear weaponry and had devised an atomic bomb that was only as large as a tennis ball. The story was picked up by news agencies across the world and soon the American President Harry Truman himself felt compelled to come out and deny the story was true.

In 1949, politicians from the Dáil, Stormont and Westminster nominated him for the Nobel Peace Prize. However, some sources quite wrongly state he was nominated for the Nobel Prize in Physiology or Medicine. He had attended the prize ceremonies in 1947 with his friend Erwin Schrödinger, most famous for his confusing thought experiment concerning quantum mechanics and possibly dead cats.

After eleven years in the city, he moved to Ghana and set up a clinic. He published two books of poetry during this time.

He died aged just forty on his way home following a speech to the United Nations on the unification of Togoland. He had been taken suddenly ill in Hamburg and apparently sent word to his wife at home that he had been poisoned. A blue plaque was erected in 2011 in his memory, at the site of his practice on Northland Road.

Bishop George Berkeley (1685-1753)

Berkeley, originally from Kilkenny, is perhaps the most prominent Irish philosopher. His major arguments involve his ideas of 'immaterialism', which proposes that physical matter does not exist in reality without first being perceived in the mind. Perhaps it is typically Irish that our major contribution to philosophy is the absurd, but difficult to refute, idea that physical objects don't really exist!

He became Dean of Derry in 1724 but spent most of his time in this post in America and England.

The University of California at Berkeley is named after him, as is a town in Massachusetts, a college and seminary at Yale University, a school in Florida and the Library at Trinity College Dublin. In Derry, a blue plaque on Bishop Street commemorates his time as Dean.

William Coppin (1805-1895)

Cork man William Coppin was a marine inventor who went to Canada at a young age to study his trade. In 1830, he met some merchants from Derry in the West Indies who commissioned him to build a boat. He decided to settle in the city when he delivered this boat. He took over a shipbuilding yard in Derry, employing up to 500 men.

His most ambitious project was an enormous steamer called the *Great Northern*. About 20,000 people turned out in Derry to see its launch, although unfortunately its first trip to London was the only voyage it ever made. Unable to find a buyer, Coppin was forced to sell it for scrap.

He experimented with various inventions for the rest of his life, including a diving suit and a method for raising sunken vessels. He is buried at St Augustine's church in Derry and is the subject of an exhibition in the Harbour Museum.

Omid Djalili (1965-)

London-born Djalili, who describes himself as the only Iranian comedian (still three more than Germany, he says), attended the University of Ulster, Coleraine in the 1980s.

He lived in a cottage in Castlerock and was described as being a 'very skilful' football player by his former coach at the university.

He graduated with a degree in English and Theatre Studies in 1988. Since then he has appeared in films like *Pirates of the Caribbean: At World's End*, *Sex and the City 2* and the 1999 Bond film *The World is Not Enough*.

Amelia Earhart (1897-?)

This famous aviator became the first woman to fly solo across the Atlantic when she landed in a field near Ballyarnett, Derry in 1932. Her destination had been Paris, but as conditions became dangerous, Earhart had been forced to land after nearly fifteen hours in the air.

She was approached by a farmer when she landed who asked, 'Have you flown far?' to which she replied, 'Just from America.'

Earhart disappeared in 1937, while attempting a round-the-world flight. She left Lae, New Guinea bound for Howland Island, near Hawaii and was never seen again. Much speculation followed, as did many searches.

Efforts have been made to rename the local airport after Earhart but the proposal was shot down when it was brought before Derry City Council. However, Rock Pigeon Club in Ballyarnett renamed itself 'Amelia Earhart Flying Club' in 2012. There is also a small museum near the site of her landing.

Ulysses S. Grant (1822-1885)

The great-grandfather of the eighteenth President of the United States, Ulysses S. Grant, was from Ballygawley, County Tyrone and had emigrated to Ohio in 1750.

President Grant, who was born at Mountpleasant Point, Ohio, embarked on a round-the-world trip and after visits to London, Paris and Spain he arrived in Dublin on 3 January 1879. He travelled to Derry several days later, where police were needed to keep the massive crowds in order.

W.M. Thackeray (1811-1863)

The novelist William Makepeace Thackeray visited Coleraine, Limavady, Ballykelly, Eglinton and Derry city in 1842. Most famous for the novel *Vanity Fair*, Thackeray was in the country mainly to make notes for his controversial book, *The Irish Sketch Book*.

During his trip, he visited a pub in Limavady, where he was bewitched by a smiling barmaid. He was so taken with 'Peg of Limavady' that he spilt his ale all over the floor. Although he said he spent very little time in the town, perhaps as little as ten minutes, memories of Peg would not leave his mind and he penned a poem about their encounter.

DESCENDENTS OF DERRY

The Nobel Prize-winning novelist John Steinbeck, who wrote *The Grapes of Wrath* and *Of Mice and Men*, visited Ballykelly and Limavady in 1952. His grandfather, Samuel Hamilton, was a Ballykelly man who emigrated to California aged just seventeen. He features prominently in Steinbeck's book *East of Eden*.

Writing in *Colliers' Magazine*, Steinbeck described how he had driven completely through Ballykelly, thinking it was much too small to be the place he was looking for. He described it, using a Texas phrase, as merely 'a wide place in the road'.

Unfortunately Steinbeck's last surviving aunt, Mary Elizabeth (known as Minnie) Hamilton, died just two years before his visit. However, he is photographed visiting the graves of his ancestors at Tamlaght Finlagan parish church.

In 2009, *Doctor Who* actor David Tennant took part in an episode of the BBC's *Who Do You Think You Are?* The show revealed that his grandmother was from Derry and his grandfather, Archie McLeod, had played football for Derry City in the 1930s and is still the highest goal scorer in the team's history.

Actor and writer Mark Gatiss – best known for his roles in The League of Gentlemen, Sherlock and Game of Thrones – also paid a visit to County Derry during an October 2015 episode of the show. Gatiss was investigating the ancestry of his mother, Winifred 'Winnie' O'Kane and visited Derry city and Dungiven as he traced his family back five generations.

In August 2017 TV presenter Fearne Cotton filmed part of her episode of Who Do You Think You Are? in Garvagh, having traced her great-great-great-great grandfather William Gilmour to the area.

The family of Stephen Foster, regarded as the father of American popular song, can be traced to Derry, as his grandfather emigrated from the area during the eighteenth century. The most famous tune he penned is undoubtedly *Camptown Races*.

The parents of Declan Donnelly, one half of TV duo Ant and Dec, are from Desertmartin.

It is recorded that several members of the Crockett family were among the defenders of Derry during the 1689 Siege. Joseph Louis Crockett is believed to have emigrated to America in around 1708. He was the great-great-grandfather of Davy Crockett, who made his name in another famous siege – The Battle of the Alamo in 1836.

Derry is also the ancestral home of several world leaders. The ancestors of James Knox Polk, the eleventh President of the United States, emigrated to North Carolina from the Coleraine area. While Polk was just starting out in the American Congress, George Canning was Prime Minister of Britain. Canning, whose father was from Garvagh, is known for having the shortest tenure of any British prime minister. He died from pneumonia after only 119 days in office.

3

PLACES

Derry is a place that is both ancient and modern. It was where the first people settled in Ireland and an early site of religious importance for pagans and later for Christians. The city was transformed from a monastic society, to the site of a battle of European importance, to a beacon of cultural diversity and innovation.

The streets and buildings of the city are steeped in history, which draws thousands of travellers each year, eager to see the sights along the walls, war zones and the water. This chapter would be much poorer without the inclusion of places from around Derry county, places that have seen the making of legends, world records and glimpses of the afterlife ...

EDUCATION

University of Ulster
The Derry campus of the University of Ulster began life as Magee College in 1865. Its founder, Martha Magee, was the widow of minister William Magee. She inherited a fortune from her brothers who died in India. As both her sons also died in the military, she donated much of her money to various causes. She gave £20,000 to the Presbyterian Church of Ireland to build a college in 1845 and died the following year.

Florence Nightingale visited Magee College in 1867. Her name appears in the visitors' book, but the purpose of her visit is not entirely clear. It appears likely she made the trip to visit her friend Agnes 'Oonagh' Jones.

The British Navy used Magee as a base during the Second World War. Recently it was discovered that they built a secret underground bunker at the college, which was not only bomb-proof but was defended with gas-protection chambers. It is believed to have acted as an important command centre during the Battle of the Atlantic.

The current Coleraine Campus was originally the site of the New University of Ulster, which was set up in 1968. The following year Magee was incorporated into this university and in 1984 the Ulster Polytechnic at Jordanstown also became part of the university.

There is a story that when *Mastermind* was filmed at the Coleraine campus, a group of students kidnapped the famous black chair and held it to ransom. When the BBC refused to pay up, the students pushed it into the River Bann.

St Columb's College

St Columb's College, founded in 1879, has had many famous people pass through its doors. Former pupils include not only two Nobel Prize winners in politician John Hume and poet Seamus Heaney, but a long list of men who are leaders in their field, from actor Gerard McSorley and broadcaster Mark McFadden to footballer Darron Gibson.

WORKHOUSES

The Poor Law Act of 1838 was enacted to help those in poverty throughout Ireland. A condition of receiving 'relief' was that recipients had to enter a workhouse and become labourers in the particular trades with which their workhouse was involved. Males and females were segregated upon entry. Conditions in the buildings were often cramped and uncomfortable and inmates had to subsist on small amounts of porridge and potatoes.

The Famine of the 1840s made conditions even worse, as the workhouses admitted more and more people. They functioned as fever hospitals at this time and diseases like dysentery and typhus were rife.

The county's first workhouse, designed to accommodate 800 inmates, opened in Derry city in November 1840. A museum was opened in the building in 1997, but closed in early 2014.

Coleraine's workhouse opened in April 1842 and was designed to accommodate 700 inmates. The site was later used as the Coleraine Hospital.

Magherafelt's workhouse was designed to house 900 inmates and was opened in March 1842. It closed in 1941, with the remaining inmates being transferred to Coleraine. The site was used as the Magherafelt and District Hospital, later the Mid-Ulster Hospital.

Limavady's workhouse first opened in March 1842, a few days after Magherafelt workhouse was opened. It is unclear what form of labour the workhouse specialised in, which varied widely from workhouse to workhouse. It has been suggested however, that the main concern of those in Limavady was either shoe making or raising pigs. The building was designed to accommodate up to 500 inmates, yet the 1901 census shows just over 100 living there.

Sightings of ghosts have often been reported at the Limavady site. Security guards said that they regularly heard crying babies in the area near the maternity ward. Sightings of nurses in old-fashioned clothes, including one with a wooden leg, have also been reported.

The BBC show *NI's Greatest Haunts* visited the workhouse in 2009. The programme showed a number of strange occurrences, including mysterious scratches that appeared on a crew member's back. A psychic also reported sensing the presence of a nurse and an 'insect' that they could not identify.

A matron and two children are said to wander the site of the Derry workhouse in the Waterside. The matron is said to be buried at the top of a flight of steps leading to a room where she left the children to suffocate. People have reported hearing children running around and one person claims to have seen a woman in white who walked through a wall.

HAUNTED HOUSES

Speaking of haunted workhouses, no Derry native is a stranger to a good ghost story. For example, a mysterious stagecoach driver, described as 'portly', is said to stop his coach and enter the White Horse Hotel near Eglinton, before disappearing.

In 2005, a house in Moneymore was reported as being haunted. It proved difficult to find tenants who would stay in the house after a mother of two forced the Housing Executive to find her a new home. She claims to have heard noises in the night and saw strange figures standing on the stairs. A neighbour went into the derelict house at one point and reported that he came across a circle of stones and an Ouija board.

Springhill House
Springhill House, near Moneymore, was built around 1680 and was the home of the Lenox-Conyngham family for several generations. The Conynghams, originally from Scotland, came to Ireland in the early seventeenth century and were granted lands during the Plantation of Ulster.

The Lenox part of the family name was added when the estate passed to Ann Conyngham, who married a man called Clotworthy Lenox. The name was adopted by their descendent Col. George Lenox.

George was on duty when he heard that his children had contracted smallpox. He was so worried that he abandoned his post and went home to Springhill, where he found that his second wife Olivia had nursed the children back to health. However, he soon heard news that he was to be court-martialled for taking his trip home. He fell into a deep depression for two years, which was exacerbated by the death of one of his daughters. One night, he took a pistol from the wall, went to what is known as the 'Blue Room' and shot himself.

Olivia apparently realised what her husband was about to do and tried to stop him, but was too late. It is her ghost that is said to haunt the house, making the same desperate attempt to save her husband over and over again.

The sightings are most commonly reported as occurring in the Blue Room. The phantom has been seen reacting in horror at the door, walking around the house dressed in black and has also been reported as checking on sleeping children that stayed in the house.

The house was bought by the National Trust in the 1950s and is open to visitors who can admire the house and grounds and perhaps catch a glimpse of the famous ghost.

DERRY CITY LANDMARKS

Derry's Walls

The famous walls were built between 1613 and 1619 under the supervision of Sir Edward Doddington. Peter Benson of London, a specialist bricklayer, was granted the contract to build the walls and would go on to become mayor.

The walls enclose an area of around thirty-two acres, measure about a mile around and are about eight feet high. They vary in width from around twelve to thirty-five feet.

Derry claims to have Europe's largest collection of cannon on the walls, with twenty guns dating from around 1590 to 1642. The most famous is Roaring Meg, a cannon that was used to defend the city during the siege. Meg got her name as a result of the deep booming sound she made when fired.

The walls originally had just four gates – Shipquay Gate, Ferryquay Gate, Butcher Gate and Bishop Gate. Other gates, including Castle Gate,

Magazine Gate and New Gate were added in the eighteenth and nineteenth centuries.

Watchtowers were added to the walls in the 1620s. Some have unusual stories behind their names, like Coward's Bastion, which was said to be one of the safest places to be during the city's siege. Hangman's Bastion is named for a man who became entangled in the very rope he was using to escape the city!

The Tower Museum is located within the walls. It opened in 1992 and has exhibitions about the history of the city and *La Trinidad Valencera*, a shipwreck from the Spanish Armada.

The Guildhall

The site where the Guildhall now stands was once in the middle of the Foyle and a place where ships moored. The land was reclaimed in the eighteenth century and the building, built in 1887, was modelled on its counterpart in London.

This building would be mostly destroyed in a fire in 1908 and after extensive rebuilding the Guildhall you see today was opened in 1912. It would be damaged again by bomb attacks in 1972.

The Guildhall has been at the centre of Derry life since it opened. Brian Friel's play *Translations* was first performed at the Guildhall with a cast including Liam Neeson and Stephen Rea. American President Bill Clinton spoke in the square outside in 1995 during his first visit to the city and gave a speech again when he returned in March 2014.

The Guildhall was also the home of the Saville Inquiry. Public hearings were conducted in the building and crowds gathered in Guildhall Square to hear the report's conclusions and to hear from relatives of those that were killed on Bloody Sunday.

Watt's Distillery

Watt's Distillery first opened on Abbey Street. Another site was opened later in the Spencer Road area of the Waterside. Together the sites could produce over two million gallons of whiskey a year. By 1887 the distillery was a world leader in whiskey production and was the largest distillery in the country.

The Tyrconnell brand was named after a racehorse owned by Andrew Alexander Watt, which won the Irish Classic in 1876, despite odds of 100 to 1. This was a popular brand across the world, particularly in the United States. It continues today as a product of the Kilbeggan Distilling Company in County Westmeath.

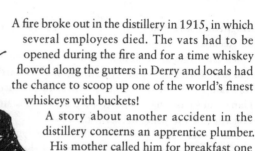

A fire broke out in the distillery in 1915, in which several employees died. The vats had to be opened during the fire and for a time whiskey flowed along the gutters in Derry and locals had the chance to scoop up one of the world's finest whiskeys with buckets!

A story about another accident in the distillery concerns an apprentice plumber. His mother called him for breakfast one morning and he was surprised to see a figure standing at the end of his bed. When he looked, it was his double, a doppelganger. It soon disappeared. The frightened lad told his mother what had happened and she was so disturbed that she would not let him go to work. That day, a boiler exploded, killing a plumber outright. The lad was saved only by the apparition at the end of his bed.

In 1921, the workers went on strike, claiming their wages were not enough. The story goes that Andrew Alexander Watt, then 68, stood on a barrel and asked the crowd if they would open the gates. When they replied in anger that they would stay shut, Watt agreed. 'Shut they are,' he said, 'and shut they shall remain!'

'Derry is now making a name for itself again in the world of quality whiskey. Quiet Man Whiskey was launched in 2015 and has been picking up international awards ever since.

St Columb's Cathedral

When the oldest building in the city was completed in 1633, a mason carved these words onto a stone plaque in the cathedral's porch.

If stones could speke,
Then London's prayse
Should sound who
Built this Church and
Cittie from the grounde.

Built under the supervision of Sir John Vaughan, it was the first Protestant Cathedral built in Britain or Ireland following the reformation.

The purpose of what is called 'The Siege Heroes' Mound' in the churchyard is something of a mystery. It may contain, or have once contained, the bones of people killed during the 1689 siege.

Austin's

Austin's in the Diamond was believed to have been the oldest department store in the world before it closed suddenly in 2016. It was opened in 1830 by Thomas Austin, making it older than Harrod's by fifteen years and Macy's of New York by twenty-five years. It was also opened eight years before Bainbridge's (now John Lewis) in Newcastle, which is often given the title of being the world's oldest.

The original store was badly damaged by a fire in 1904 and the current building was built later that year. The fire also spread to the town hall in The Diamond, causing it to be destroyed. There are plans to redevelop the building, with suggestions that it could host a new restaurant, coffee shop and cocktail bar.

AROUND THE COUNTY

City of Derry Airport

Despite its name, the airport that serves the county is actually about seven miles away from the city, near Eglinton. It was originally built as an airbase, RAF Eglinton, during the Second World War. The airport mainly offers flights to locations within the United Kingdom, like Manchester, Edinburgh and Bristol.

The airport has had problems with 'bird strikes' in recent years. In 2009, a plane bound for Birmingham was forced to land after being struck by a

flock of birds soon after take-off. The airport stressed that policies are in place to manage this issue, but it can be difficult to contain birds in the area.

The airport has also been the site where several world records were set. In 1987 the Virgin Atlantic Flyer landed 4 miles away from the airport. It was the world's largest hot air balloon at the time and earned Richard Branson the record for the first transatlantic flight in a hot air balloon.

In August 2013, Tom Lackey from the West Midlands became the world's oldest wing walker when he was strapped to the wings of a plane for the eighty-one-minute journey from Castle Kennedy, Scotland to City of Derry Airport. Tom, then 93, endured speeds of 75mph on his trip. He performs stunts like this to raise money for charity, following the death of his wife, Isabel. He also carries her picture with him during each stunt.

The RAF also opened a base in Ballykelly during the Second World War. It was handed over to the army in 1971 and became known as Shackleton Barracks. In 2006 a Ryanair jet carrying thirty-nine passengers from Liverpool accidentally landed at the Ballykelly base – six miles away from its destination of City of Derry airport.

Downhill

Frederick Hervey, the Fourth Earl of Bristol and Bishop of Derry, built several interesting buildings in the Magilligan region. His home in the area, Downhill House, was built in the late 1770s. Hervey turned it into an extravagant mansion and housed his impressive collection of artworks there, including paintings by Rembrandt and Caravaggio. The house was badly damaged in a fire in 1851 and has deteriorated since, but the ruins can still be seen today.

Hervey also built Mussenden Temple in 1785, at the top of a 120-foot cliff. It meant to serve as a summer library and was modelled on the Temple of Vesta, which he had admired in Rome. It was named after Hervey's cousin Frideswide Mussenden, who died before the temple was finished, aged just twenty-two.

At a time when it was illegal for Catholic priests to say Mass, the Earl Bishop allowed Catholics to use a room underneath the temple to worship in secret. If discovered, his compassion could have had grave consequences for all concerned. Some visitors to the temple have reported witnessing unexplainable things, like a patch of blood that seems to appear on the floor and then disappears again.

Not far from the temple is Magilligan Strand. In the 1820s, the area was used as part of the baseline to conduct the Ordnance Survey of Ireland. It started at a point called 'North Station' and stretched for more than six miles to 'South Station' in Ballykelly. This line was what all other references in Ireland were measured against. The Ordnance Survey would move from county to county, conducting measurements for another eighteen years before the mapping of the island was complete.

One of the first aeroplane flights in Ireland also took place in Magilligan. Harry Ferguson managed to fly a home-made aeroplane on his first attempt in 1909, flying 130 feet at a height of nine feet.

Ferguson, from County Down, would later found a company that built tractors. This company merged with Massey-Harris in 1953 to form the Massey-Ferguson Company. I wonder how many people think that William Ferguson-Massey, the Prime Minister of New Zealand born in Limavady, was somehow involved with the tractor company. Or how many from Limavady really know that the Ferguson-Masseys have nothing at all to do with Massey-Ferguson but that the company was really formed, in part, by an engineer who designed and flew a plane just a few miles away in Magilligan?

The Martello Tower

The British built towers in the nineteenth century to defend coasts against possible French invaders. Around seventy of these were built in Ireland, including one in Magilligan. The tower is well equipped to handle an attack, with thirteen-foot sandstone walls, storage space for food, a well, and a furnace designed to heat cannon balls before firing.

The most famous of the 'Martellos', as they are sometimes called, is in Sandycove, in south County Dublin. James Joyce lived there briefly and the tower is the setting for the opening chapter of *Ulysses*. Today it serves as a museum about the writer.

The Glenshane Pass

The Ponderosa Bar was established as Buchanan's in 1858 just off the Glenshane Pass. It was named after the bar in the TV show *Bonanza* in the 1960s.

It claims the title of the highest bar in Ireland, although there are other bars that dispute the Ponderosa's claim. According to Ordnance Survey maps however, the Ponderosa is 946 feet above sea level. The other main contender for the title is Johnny Fox's in the Dublin Mountains, which is only 912 feet above sea level.

In September 1943, an American Cassna 'Bobcat' plane crashed near the pub, killing all three men on board. The men, including Commodore Logan, the Commander of US Naval Forces in Northern Ireland, were on their way to meet General Dwight Eisenhower in London.

Guy L. Wilson Daffodil Garden

This garden at the University of Ulster, Coleraine is named after local daffodil breeder Guy L. Wilson. When the flowers are in bloom, around March or April, there are over 1,000 varieties of daffodils on display, some of which have been donated from countries around the world, including Holland and New Zealand.

In 2002 the university also unveiled the Millennium Arboretum which contains more than 100 varieties of trees.

Bellaghy Bawn

Built during the plantation in the seventeenth century, Bellaghy Bawn is a fortified house. It has housed items related to local poet Seamus Heaney for some time, including manuscripts and his old school bag. These items were made available for the public to view in 1996.

There have been rumours that the building is haunted. In 2009 it featured on the BBC TV show *NI's Greatest Haunts*. Ghost hunters carried out experiments that revealed unusual knocks and voices in the house, while a psychic spoke about the spirit of an angry soldier inhabiting the house.

RIVERS

Foyle

The eighty-mile long River Foyle begins in what is now the Republic of Ireland, in Lifford, County Donegal. It then flows through Strabane and Derry city before reaching Lough Foyle.

The river is considered good for angling, due to the presence of large numbers of Atlantic salmon. It is also a popular place to practise sports like water-skiing and canoeing. In 2014 ships competing in the Clipper Round the World Race sailed along the river as part of the route. The ships were warmly welcomed and it is believed the race will return to Derry in the near future.

In 1977 a whale swam into the Foyle. It became confused while hanging around the Craigavon Bridge and could not figure out how to return to the sea. Eventually he had to be directed back to open water. He was named Dopey Dick by residents, as he couldn't find his own way home.

The river has been patrolled by Foyle Search and Rescue since 1993. The charity aims to prevent suicide and support families in Derry City and they have rescued more than 350 from the dangers of the Foyle – one of the coldest and fastest flowing rivers in Europe. The team is universally respected and admired in Derry for their difficult work, which has included the recovery of over 130 bodies from the river.

Moyola

The Moyola River begins in the Sperrin Mountains, runs through the Moyola Estate near Castledawson before continuing to Lough Neagh. It is known for being a good source of brown trout, although in recent years there have been serious concerns about the pollution of the river.

It is considered to be an important part of the 'Heaney country' as the river is near to the poet's childhood home of Bellaghy. It was a regular feature in his poetry throughout his life

Roe

The River Roe begins high in the Sperrin Mountains before flowing through Dungiven, Burnfoot, Limavady and Myroe. It is considered a good spot for trout and salmon fishing.

Bann

The River Bann is the longest river in Northern Ireland. It begins as the Upper Bann in the Mourne Mountains and flows into Lough Neagh at

Bannfoot, County Armagh. The Lower Bann flows from Lough Neagh at Toome, County Antrim, through Kilrea and Coleraine to the Atlantic at Portstewart. The entire length of the river, including the section at Lough Neagh, is estimated at being ninety miles long.

It is home to salmon and eel fisheries and is also popular with those interested in water sports. It has also served as a marker for religious and political divisions in Northern Ireland. The west of the Bann is predominately rural and Catholic, while major Protestant areas and Northern Ireland's main industrial area around Belfast, lie east of the Bann.

During the 1641 Rebellion a large number of Protestants were forced into the river at Portadown and drowned.

WHAT'S IN A NAME?

The city's name has had many different variations over the years, all related to *doire*, the Irish word meaning oak grove. The city has been called Doire Calgach and Doire Colmcille.

The prefix London was added to the anglicised name Derry in 1613. Today, both Derry and Londonderry are used to refer to the city or county. There are endless arguments about which name is right or official which result in references to history (about which came first), legal matters (the name used by courts, council and government) and culture (names used by residents of the area.)

In general, the guideline when speaking about the area is respect. Although somewhat strange to outsiders, the ideal situation would be the ability for two people to discuss city or county with one choosing to refer to it as Derry and the other as Londonderry, with neither person seeking to correct the other.

Some use both names 'Derry-Londonderry' which can be a bit cumbersome. This name gives rise to another, 'Stroke City,' referring to the dash separating the name. This was coined by radio presenter Gerry Anderson. Finally, there is the 'Maiden City,' which refers to the fact that the city walls were not breached during the Siege of Derry.

PLACE NAMES

A great deal of the towns in County Derry take their names from clans or families important in the area, including Dawson (Castledawson), O'Ceallaigh or O'Kelly (Ballykelly) and McGuigan (Ballymaguigan).

Many others are named for geographical features such as Articlave from the Irish *Ard an Chléibh*, meaning 'height of the basket'. The term basket here can also refer to the framework of ribs – so may also signify breast or bosom. The name then may refer to a basket-shaped feature or the 'bosom' of a hill in the area.

Yet, several names are unique and peculiar. Here are some of the strangest names and where they are believed to have originated.

Ballyclose – an area of Limavady, means 'town of the ears'. This comes from a dispute between local clans. It began when the chieftain of the O'Mullans drowned two young McCloskey boys they had caught hunting in their territory. The McCloskeys retaliated, with the help of the O'Cahans and when the O'Mullans were defeated the captured warriors had their ears cut off.

Another battle involving the O'Cahans and the O'Mullans, ended badly again for the O'Mullans. This time it was their heads that were cut off and were buried at a place called Knock-Na-Ginn, which can be translated as the hill of heads.

Banagher – Beannchar – the rather specific 'spiked palisade surrounding a monastery'.

Culmore – An Chúil Mhór – 'the big secluded spot'.

Cushcapal in Banagher Glen – Cos Capaill – 'leg of the horse'.

Dungiven – Dún Geimhin – 'fort of (the) hide'. If this is the correct interpretation, hides and skins may have been stored here.

Limavady – Léim an Mhadaidh – 'leap of the dog'.

Moneyneany – Móin na nIonadh – 'bog of the wonders'. The name refers to the area as a place associated with fairies and magic.

Several place names clearly take their name from professions or the people with which the area was associated.

Benbradagh – An Bhinn Bhradach – Often translated as 'the treacherous peak' but has also been called 'cliff of the robbers', 'cliff of lying in wait' and 'the hill of thieves'. The treacherous aspect may have it roots in a local story of a woman of ill repute called Maeve or 'Maevebradagh'.

Maeve is referenced again in the Sperrins with the full name of Sawel Mountain. Sawel or Samhail means 'likeness'. The peak's full name is Samhail Phite Méabha meaning 'likeness to Maeve's vulva'. This strange description may refer to a hollow on the side of the mountain but also calls to mind the 'sheela na gig' fertility carvings found across Ireland.

Castlerock – Although it seems like a name that refers to the local landscape, the village actually takes its name from a shipwreck. In 1826 Robert Castles perished with the crew of a ship called the *Trader of Greenock*. Supposedly the area is named for this man and the rock that sank his ship.

Draperstown is a special case. First of all, the current village is actually the second Draperstown in the county. The name derives from the Worshipful Company of Drapers from London, who originally gave the name to Moneymore. Several older names survive among the locals, including Ballinascreen, the 'land of the shrine'.

Gulladuff – Guala Dhubh – Several translations including 'black shoulders' and 'black forks', referring to hills in the area.

OVERSEAS

As the people of Derry spread out across the globe, they brought their names with them. You could find yourself thousands of miles from Ireland and all of a sudden driving into a Derry, Londonderry or Coleraine.

Aside from more than a thousand places across Ireland featuring Derry in the name, including places in counties Laois, Tipperary and Down, there are many further afield including six Derrys in the United States, including one in New Hampshire that was the home of poet Robert Frost.

There are eleven Londonderrys spread out across England, Australia and America. There is also the isolated Cape Londonderry in Western Australia and Londonderry Island off the coast of Chile.

There are also quite a few Coleraines and Colerains in the United States, along with a Colrain in Massachusetts, as well as in Canada and Australia. The Treaty of Colerain was signed in Colerain, Georgia in 1796. It was an agreement between the United States Government and representatives of the Indian Muscogee, or Creek, Nation.

PARALLEL WORLDS

Oddly enough, the famous horror writer Stephen King has invented two towns that have links to Derry. His town of Derry, Maine is the setting for several novels, including *Bag of Bones* and *11/23/66* and is the home of creepy clown Pennywise from *It*.

Another setting for his novels is Castle Rock, just like the seaside village. This area is the setting for novels like *Cujo* and *The Dead Zone*, as well as the short story *The Body,* later adapted into the film *Stand by Me*.

4

CRIME AND PUNISHMENT

Derry has its fair share of criminals and scoundrels. Some are relatively harmless and a bit foolish, some simply unfortunate and some have been dubbed 'evil' for their terrible actions. As with everywhere, hidden among the decent, hard-working people are predators eyeing up opportunities to steal, taking note of the vulnerable, making plans to kill …

Both city and county has been deeply marked by the violence of the Troubles, but those events are far from the only crimes of note in the area. Here we take a look at some of the more unusual cases in Derry's history, from the undeniably gruesome to the laughably ridiculous.

VANDALS IN THE GRAVEYARD

Kevin O'Kane, the caretaker of a cemetery in Claudy, became concerned when ornamental stones began to disappear from a number of graves. He was approached by family members of the deceased who were understandably distressed and asked him to catch the thieves.

O'Kane kept watch on the graves and before long the culprits reappeared. Crows arrived and completely stripped graves of their stones. The families were relieved and took precautions to prevent the crows bothering the graves of their loved ones again, by laying down marble slabs. 'If they can lift that,' said Kevin, 'by God, they are strong crows.'

THE BAG MAN

Early one morning in 2013, the staff at the Spar convenience store in Limavady were confronted by a man carrying a large kitchen knife. The burglar had entered the shop with a plastic bag over his head as a disguise and waited patiently in the queue before making his demand.

As if this wasn't bad enough, he was an 'almost daily' customer and was instantly recognised by staff when he attempted to take money from the till.

Although the man said that his actions were a prank, his lengthy criminal record stood against him. Despite being just 20, he had already stacked up seventy-one previous criminal convictions. He pleaded guilty to aggravated burglary, served fourteen months in prison and was banned from going within fifty metres of the shop for five years.

REPRESENTING THE BUTCHER OF BAGHDAD

Saddam Hussein was the President of Iraq from 1979 until he was deposed in 2003. He was known as a brutal dictator who presided over widespread torture and unjustified imprisonment and is believed to have been responsible for the deaths of more than 250,000 of his citizens. He was captured by American forces in Tikrit, near Baghdad in December 2003 and was put on trial in October 2005.

One of the dictator's solicitors was Des Doherty from Derry. Doherty blasted the proceedings, claiming they were illegal and that the legitimacy of the court would not stand up to international criticism. He said that the trial, held in Baghdad, was biased and had been 'largely funded by the US and was heavily staffed by US personnel'.

Hussein was later convicted of crimes against humanity and sentenced to death. He was executed by hanging in December 2006.

HALF-HANGED MCNAUGHTON

John McNaughton was born into a wealthy family in 1722 but managed to gamble away most of his inheritance and build up substantial debts. He turned to a childhood friend, Donegal MP Andrew Knox, who brought him into his home, Prehen House.

Knox's 15-year-old daughter Mary Anne became enamoured with McNaughton and it was rumoured that McNaughton tricked her into a secret marriage, so that he might claim her substantial dowry to fund his habit.

Andrew Knox was outraged at this development between his old friend and his daughter and forbade the couple from having any contact. He intended to spirit Mary Anne away to Dublin, far away from McNaughton.

McNaughton lay in wait for their carriage and fired shots inside in an attempt to abduct Mary Anne. Sadly, one of the shots hit Mary Anne, wounding her mortally.

He was soon arrested and sentenced to death by hanging. Yet when it came to his execution, the rope broke. Although this gave him an opportunity to escape, he returned to be executed claiming he didn't wish to be remembered as a 'half-hanged' man. He was hanged a second time, this time successfully.

His presence is said to linger at Prehen House; in one bedroom in particular some people have reported a figure which gets into bed beside them. The house appeared on the BBC show *NI's Greatest Haunts* in 2010. Those involved in the show reported seeing a dark figure in the house and recorded a series of knocks they believed were in response to their questions. A medium who visited the house felt that the spirit of Andrew Knox had become trapped and that the team helped to set it free.

THE HIGHWAYMEN

After Shane Crossagh O'Mullan saw his family evicted from their land near Faughanvale, he rounded up a gang of men in similar circumstances to take revenge on the landlords in the area.

The gang of outlaws carried out many attacks around the Sperrins and O'Mullan became a sort of Robin Hood figure. In one tale he outwits General Napier, who had been pursuing O'Mullan for some time, by piling turf on hills surrounding the road, creating the illusion that the general's troops were surrounded by armed men. He shot the general's horse himself, then the threat of his turf army allowed O'Mullan to relieve Napier and his men of their weapons and uniforms. The general and his troops were then made to walk to Derry in what little clothing they had left.

His exploits caught up to him eventually and he was executed in the 1720s. His memory has lived on though, as the Glenshane Pass is named after him.

A similar figure is Cushy Glen, who is believed to have come from somewhere near Magilligan. He seems to have been more bloodthirsty than O'Mullan and would eye up travellers in Coleraine to follow, attack and rob along the isolated mountain road towards Limavady.

This road, today known as the Windyhill road, was once known as the Murderhole Road, apparently after a pit into which the highwayman would toss the bodies of his victims. A statue of Cushy Glen can now be found on the road, watching travellers pass, with a knife in his hand.

THE KILLER DOCTOR

John Bodkin Adams was born in Randalstown, County Antrim in 1899. The family moved to Ballinderry when he was still a small child and he went on to attend the Coleraine Academic Institution before studying medicine at Queen's University, Belfast.

He moved to Eastbourne in England to work as a general practitioner with a Christian practice in 1922. At that time, the seaside town had many affluent retired residents, mostly women, that were private patients of Adams and his colleagues.

In 1956, the police began to investigate the doctor, who had been involved in a large number of suspicious deaths. He had been named by hundreds of his patients as a beneficiary in their wills and the police suspected Adams was murdering his patients to collect the money. He was tried for only one murder, that of Edith Morell who died in 1951 at the age of 81.

Morell became a patient of Adams in 1948 after she suffered a stroke. Within days of becoming her doctor, Adams was injecting Morell with large doses of morphine and dia-morphine (heroin), which were well over the recommended doses. Edith quickly became dependent on these drugs and of course, on the doctor who provided them. It wasn't long before Adams brought in a solicitor who made changes to Morell's will, leaving the dining-room silver, a Rolls-Royce and her house to Adams.

He admitted before his trial that he had helped to 'ease the passage' of some of his patients. Testimonies given during the trial also revealed that Adams preferred wealthy elderly women as patients. He often prescribed strong drugs to patients and asked nurses to leave the room when administering injections. On one occasion he booked a post-mortem before a patient had even died.

However, although it was clear that Morell had died an unnatural death, the jury acquitted Adams of murder as they felt there was not enough evidence to suggest he had administered excessive quantities of drugs.

He was later convicted for forging prescriptions and lying on cremation certificates. For that he was struck off the medical register and fined £2,400. However, he could still practise medicine (but could not declare himself qualified or prescribe restricted/dangerous drugs) and returned to treat many of his former patients in Eastbourne. Reinstated after four years, he worked and lived on in the town until his death in 1983.

Some believe that the case of Adams and the belief that he got away with murder may have inspired another other notorious killer doctor – Harold Shipman.

PROWLER ON THE LOOSE

Gerald McLaughlin, a farmer from Feeny, has lost more than 400 of his sheep over the past twenty years in very disturbing circumstances. Too often he has gone out to his fields to find young lambs that have had their tongues cut out by a mysterious prowler.

No one has ever been caught in the act despite the amount of incidents and the police are reportedly baffled. A theory was put forward that birds may be responsible for the lambs losing their tongues, but McLaughlin responds to that by pointing out that only his flock seems to be affected.

The perpetrators do not kill the lambs, but rather they are left to bleed to death or they need to be put down.

RAAD

Republican Action Against Drugs (RAAD) is a vigilante group that began in Derry city in 2008. They claim that they have no political agenda and are committed only to removing drug dealers from the local community.

To that end they have attacked many alleged drug dealers in Derry and Donegal, having planted bombs at their homes and kidnapped people to endure punishment shootings, usually in the legs, as a part of the process known as 'knee-capping'. One mother has spoken about being forced to take her son to a certain location in order to be shot. She said that she felt it was right to co-operate with RAAD because if they had resisted, her son may have been killed.

RAAD say that they monitor suspected dealers and until June 2010 they offered an 'amnesty' which allowed them to continue living normal lives, having proved that they have stopped dealing drugs.

The organisation claims that their intervention is necessary as the PSNI are not addressing the issue of drug dealing in the area, yet RAAD have, in the past, also attacked the owners of head shops that sell 'legal highs', despite the fact that the shops were operating within the law.

RAAD's actions have largely been met with horror by the overwhelming majority of people in Derry and numerous rallies have been held in protest against their violence.

The organisation, which has had links to the Provisional IRA since it began, merged with other dissident republican groups in 2012. This new group, which includes members of the Real IRA, has been responsible for the murder of a prison officer and have also launched attacks on police stations and vehicles in Derry city.

CICILY JACKSON

In 1725 Cicily Jackson was accused of 'petty treason'. In those days, petty treason could mean the killing of a husband or master, but in Jackson's case, she was accused of having murdered her own child.

For her crime she was burned at the stake at Bishopsgate on St Patrick's Day. She is believed to have been the last person to be burned at the stake in Derry.

In recent years, University of Ulster lecturer John Thompson has looked into Cicily's back story. She worked as a cook for the Anglican Bishop of Derry, William Nicholson. Thompson believes that the father of Cicily's baby was the Bishop's nephew, James Nicholson.

James had recently been ordained and the revelation of an illegitimate child would undoubtedly stain the family's reputation. This research

has led Thompson to believe that there may have been more to the death of the infant than the traditional story.

STEALING A SEA GOD

A £10,000 statue of the sea god Manannán Mac Lir was stolen from the top of Binevenagh Mountain in January 2015. It would have taken several men hours with angle grinders to remove the statue from its base.

As the statue was made of out fibreglass and stainless steel, it could not be sold for scrap. The motives for the theft appear instead to be religious. The thieves left a wooden cross in place of the pagan figure with the words 'You shall have no other gods before me' written on it.

The story quickly spread worldwide and the chief executive of Limavady Borough Council, Liam Flanagan, reported that he had received letters of support and offers to donate money from the United States, Canada and New Zealand. Plans were set in place to commission a replacement statue from the original artist.

Around a month after the theft, the sculpture was found badly damaged by ramblers around 300 yards from where it had stood.

THE BODYSNATCHER

It is not clear where William Hare was born. Some sources claim he was originally from Newry, but others say that he was a Derry man. Along with his partner in crime, William Burke from Tyrone, he has become infamous for murdering innocent people in Scotland so that he could sell their corpses.

The pair first met in Edinburgh in the early nineteenth century after they both emigrated from Ireland. At the time there was a demand among the city's medical schools for cadavers for examination. This led to the rise of people known as 'resurrectionists' who would find dead bodies, one way or another.

Burke and Hare became friends and went into business together as bodysnatchers. They murdered sixteen people in Edinburgh in 1828 before selling their bodies to Dr Robert Knox to be used in his classes and in medical research. They would invite their victims for a drink and then smother them when they became intoxicated. Their prey included young children, pensioners and even a mentally disabled young man known as 'Daft Jamie'.

When they were caught, the police feared that the two men would both deny any guilt and blame the other entirely, meaning neither could be convicted nor punished. Their solution was to offer Hare the chance to save himself by testifying against Burke, who was believed to be the true brains behind the operation. Hare wasted little time in condemning his partner to death by hanging, in front of over 25,000 people in 1829. Burke's skeleton is displayed to this day in the Anatomy Museum at the University of Edinburgh. A book believed to be bound in his skin is also kept at the museum.

Hare disappeared after Burke's execution and nobody knows what became of him. He may even have made his way home to Derry. His wife Margaret had also been part of the trial and afterwards was said to be heading for Derry, via a ship bound for Belfast. Perhaps he returned to the city, or to some smaller village and lived a quiet life, perhaps taking a stroll every now and then around the local graveyards at night?

The pair have featured in many films. Over the years, Hare has been portrayed by Andy Serkis, Donald Pleasence and Stephen Rae.

It was reported in October 1888 that a man arrested in Limavady was suspected to be Jack the Ripper. The man was arrested because a constable felt he fit the description of the Ripper and was described as having an American accent, looking 'travel-stained' and wearing a 'slouched hat'.

5

CULTURE AND THE ARTS

Derry has always been an extremely fertile place for all of the creative arts. There is scarcely a field of artistic expression that does not have at least one person from Derry who is prominent on the world stage. The local scene is also vibrant as festivals, performances and exhibitions are held across the city and county.

This chapter looks back on Derry's legends of art, writing and music and looks forward to singers, artists and festivals that are just getting started.

MUSIC

'Danny Boy'

'Danny Boy' is one of the most famous songs in the world and has been covered by Elvis Presley, Johnny Cash and Eva Cassidy. The lyrics were composed by English lawyer Frederic Weatherly in 1910. However, the origins of the melody prove to be more elusive.

The traditional story goes that Jane Ross heard a blind fiddler playing a tune known as the 'Londonderry Air' while walking in Limavady in 1851. She recorded the tune and sent it to music collector George Petrie. The melody was then published in his 1855 book *The Ancient Music of Ireland*.

The blind fiddler is believed to have been Jimmy McCurry, from Myroe. Ross is said to have asked him to play the tune over and over until she had taken down the whole song. She then gave him a coin for his trouble, but when he checked it against his lips he discovered it was a florin rather than the customary penny. Ross refused to take the coin back and told McCurry that he had earned it by playing such a beautiful tune.

The identity of the melody's composer is the subject of much debate. The composer could well have been one of two blind harpers from County Derry. It might seem unusual that all of the musicians related to the song are blind, but it was once common in Ireland and some other European countries for blind or disabled people to be taught an instrument so that they might support themselves.

Ruaidhri Dáll O'Cahan is believed to have been born in the early seventeenth century. He lost his sight at a young age and acquired the nickname Dáll, which is the Irish word for blind. He is said to have travelled to Scotland as a harpist and there impressed various nobles including King James VI, who invited him to play for the Scottish court.

Surviving songs that are attributed to him include *Tabhair Dom do Lamh* (Give me your hand), which is still popular today and has been performed by The Chieftains, Sir James Galway and Planxty.

It has been suggested that O'Cahan was the original composer of the melody of 'Danny Boy'. In one version of the story, the tune – here called *O'Cahan's Lament* – came to him in a dream and was a lament for the destruction of the O'Cahan clan.

He is said to have drunk too much one evening and went for a walk along the River Roe. Servants from the castle searched for him by following the sound of his harp, but when they found him he was unconscious and the music was being played by 'mysterious invisible fingers'. When he regained consciousness he remembered the song and managed to recreate it for guests at the castle.

Donnchadh Ó Hamsaigh, also known as Denis Hempson, was born at the end of the seventeenth century. His parents are believed to be have been both from Magilligan. He is said to have been blinded by smallpox at the age of three. He was brought up near Garvagh and was taught to play the harp by local musicians. He was given the 'Downhill Harp' by Councillor Canning, which he played throughout his life. This harp was bought by Guinness in 1963 and is displayed in their Storehouse Museum today.

Ó Hamsaigh is regarded as the last harper to play in the 'old way' by using his long fingernails to pluck the strings. This is just one reason which brought him to the attention of Edward Bunting at the 1792 Belfast Harp Festival, which the harpist attended at the age of 97.

Bunting, a folk music collector, noted down several of Ó Hamsaigh's tunes, including one called *Aisling an Óigfhir*, 'The young man's dream', which is strikingly similar to the melody of today's 'Danny Boy'. Bunting published this song in 1796, more than fifty years before Jane Ross's discovery of the 'Londonderry Air'.

If the song is indeed one and the same, it appears unlikely that it was composed by Ó Hamsaigh. One of his early teachers is believed to have been Bridget O'Cahan, a relative of Ruaidhri Dáll. Perhaps he learned *O'Cahan's Lament* from her?

Ó Hamsaigh spent his later years in Magilligan, where he played for the Earl Bishop Frederick Hervey. He died in 1807 (apparently at the age of 112!) and was buried at St Aidan's church, Magilligan.

Phil Coulter

Coulter grew up in Derry city and attended St Columb's College. Aged just twenty-three, he wrote Ireland's debut entry for the 1965 Eurovision Song Contest, 'Walking the Streets in the Rain'. The song finished sixth in the contest.

He later teamed up with Glaswegian Bill Martin, with whom he wrote 'Puppet on a String', the song which took Sandie Shaw to victory at Eurovision in 1967. The pair also wrote 'Congratulations' for Cliff Richard, who finished second in the 1968 contest. They would later go on to write songs for stars like the Bay City Rollers and Elvis Presley.

Coulter and Martin suspected foul play following the results of the 1968 contest, where they just missed out on the historic chance of having two winning songs in consecutive years. A Spanish documentary has alleged that dictator Francisco Franco bought votes and ensured that Spain's entry *La La La* was the winner.

In addition to working with Planxty, Christy Moore and Celtic Thunder, Coulter is known for writing some of the songs that The Dubliners are best remembered for. Luke Kelly's covers of Coulter's 'Scorn not his Simplicity' and 'The Town I Loved So Well' rank very highly among the greatest of Irish music.

Coulter also composed 'Ireland's Call', the anthem used by the Irish rugby team when playing international matches.

Peter Cunnah

Cunnah, the lead singer of D:Ream, from Derry city, shot to fame with the band's number one hit 'Things Can Only Get Better'. The song became an anthem for the 1990s and was chosen as the Labour Party's campaign song for the 1997 election. Peter Cunnah went on the campaign trail with Tony Blair and was once told by John Prescott that he was bloody fed up with the hit song he had to sing so many times.

The band, which had once featured physics professor and television presenter Brian Cox, released two albums and had several top twenty singles before they split in 1997. They reformed in 2008 and three years later released the album *In Memory Of...*

Dana

Dana Rosemary Scallon (then Brown) was raised in Derry's Bogside. She shot to fame in 1970 when she won that year's Eurovision Song Contest with the song 'All Kinds of Everything'. Dana was still a teenager when the song went to number one in charts around the world.

She has had a long music career, releasing more than twenty albums between 1970 and 2012. She moved into politics in the 1990s and served as an MEP for Connacht-Ulster from 1999-2004 as an Independent.

She has twice campaigned to become the President of Ireland. She finished third in the 1997 election behind Fine Gael's Mary Banotti and Mary McAleese of Fianna Fáil, who would hold the post until 2011. Dana ran for election again in the 2011 presidential election, finishing sixth behind Michael D. Higgins and Derry's Martin McGuinness, running for Sinn Féin.

Cara Dillon

Cara Dillon was brought up in a very musical family in Dungiven. Her sister Mary is a popular folk singer in her own right, both as a solo artist and as a member of tradional band Déanta.

In 1995, she was picked to join folk 'super-group' Equation and signed with Warner Brothers. The band would eventually break up, and after struggling to satisfy Warner Brothers, Dillon and her future husband Sam Lakeman quietly recorded an album themselves. The eponymous *Cara Dillon* became a big hit and cemented Dillon's reputation on the folk scene.

In 2010 her album *Hill of Thieves*, named after Benbradagh Mountain, won Best Album at BBC Radio 2's Folk Awards. The same year, she was approached by Disney to contribute songs to one of their films. The songs, 'Summer's Just Begun' and 'Come Flying With Me', feature on the soundtrack of *Tinker Bell and the Great Fairy Rescue*.

Dillon was surprised to find how popular her music was when touring China, selling out venues in four cities. Someone later told Cara that at least part of her fame is due to the fact that her first few albums are used to teach English to students. She released her seventh album, *Wanderer*, in 2017 .

Fighting with Wire

The second famous Cahir O'Doherty from Derry decided to form a rock band called Fighting with Wire rather than burn the city to the ground like his namesake 400 years earlier. In addition to touring the United Kingdom and Ireland, the band have played Oxegen, BBC Radio One Big Weekend and the Download Festival. The band decided to split up in February 2013.

General Fiasco

Formed in 2007, this band from Bellaghy started out supporting Fighting with Wire. After being nominated for Best British Newcomer at the 2010 Kerrang! Awards the band played T in the Park and Glastonbury. They also played an important part in the celebrations as the Olympic torch passed through Northern Ireland in 2012. Following two albums the band cancelled their UK tour and went on hiatus in January 2013.

Ciaran Gribbin

Gribbin, from Castledawson, began writing and performing music from a young age. After college he was part of the band Leya for seven years. The band split in 2009 and Gribbin – under the name Joe Echo – had the opportunity to work with Paul McCartney and Snow Patrol, among others. He also wrote and recorded all the original songs for the soundtrack of the film *Killing Bono*.

In 2010, Gribbin co-wrote the song 'Celebration' for Madonna, which earned him a Grammy nomination. The following year, he was selected to be the new lead singer of Australian band INXS, stepping into the shoes of the late Michael Hutchence.

Gribbin also contributed the song 'Hey Baby Doll' to the film *Danny Collins,* which was sung in the film by Al Pacino. He is also working on solo projects.

Henry McCullough

Guitarist McCullough, a Portstewart native, is best known for being a member of Wings with Paul McCartney.

He toured America with the band and played lead guitar on hits like 'My Love' and Bond theme, 'Live and Let Die'.

His vibrant career also led him to tour with Jimi Hendrix and play at Woodstock in 1969 with Joe Cocker, as the only Irishman to perform at the legendary festival. His voice can also be heard at the end of the track 'Money' on Pink Floyd's album, *The Dark Side of the Moon*.

McCullough suffered a serious heart attack in November 2012, which led several media outlets to wrongly report that he had died. Many musicians have raised money to help fund his continued care. A fundraising concert was held in Dublin's Vicar Street with contributions from Christy Moore, John Spillane and Mick Flannery, among others. Van Morrison also stepped in to ensure McCullough could

have a wet room installed in his home. Henry passed away in June 2016. Beatles legend Paul McCartney paid tribute to McCullough when he heard the news, saying 'He was a pleasure to work with, a super-talented musician with a lovely sense of humour.'

Johnny McDaid

Culmore's Johnny McDaid, a pianist, guitarist and singer, joined Snow Patrol in 2011, while the band was recording their sixth album, *Fallen Empires*.

In January 2013, McDaid and Snow Patrol bandmate Gary Lightbody performed at the 'Sons & Daughters' concerts, which opened Derry's year of celebrations as the UK City of Culture.

Later that year McDaid began dating *Friends* star Courteney Cox. The couple announced their engagement in June 2014. The actress, who also featured in the *Scream* films and the show *Cougar Town,* has been described as 'a wee pet' by McDaid's mum Pauline. McDaid helped write Ed Sheeran's 2014 album 'X', including the songs 'Bloodstream' and 'Photograph'. Sheeran's 2017 song 'Shape of You', which topped the charts in the UK and US was also co-written by McDaid. In an interview with *The New York Times* McDaid revealed that the song's title comes from the common Derry phrase.

Jimmy McShane

McShane left Derry for a London stage school before discovering Milan's underground dance scene. He became the frontman of New Wave band Baltimora. Their 1985 song 'Tarzan Boy' was a hit in countries around the world, particularly in France and the United States. However, the band struggled to produce songs of similar success following the hit.

When McShane was diagnosed with AIDS in 1994 he returned to Derry from Milan. He died in March 1995 and was buried in Derry's City Cemetery.

SOAK

The stage name of Bridie Monds-Watson comes from a portmanteau of the words soul and folk. She started her musical career at just fourteen, playing in a band with her friends in Derry. She released two EPs in 2012 when she was sixteen. *Trains* and *Sea Creatures* were both well received and brought her to national prominence. She has toured with George Ezra, appeared on RTÉ's *Other Voices* and played major festivals like Electric Picnic and Glastonbury. Her second album *Grim Town* was released in 2019. She has also contributed music to animated TV show *Moomin Valley.*

The Undertones

Derry's famous punk band was formed by five friends in 1975. By 1978 they were playing regular gigs in Derry and decided to approach Belfast man Terri Hooley who helped them make their first record, the four-song *Teenage Kicks* EP.

The band sent a copy of the record to BBC Radio 1 DJ John Peel and received a major boost when he championed their music, particularly the song 'Teenage Kicks'. He would later say that the song was his favourite of all time.

Before long the band were appearing on *Top of the Pops* and supporting punk legends *The Clash* in the United States. They released four albums and had many singles, like 'Here Comes the Summer', in the charts before splitting up in 1983.

The band reformed in 1999 with singer Fergal Sharkey replaced by Paul McLoone. Since their reunion they have released two more albums and performed at Glastonbury.

REALITY TV STARS

Derry natives have also performed well on reality TV shows like *The X Factor*. While still a pupil at Thornhill College, Nadine Coyle took part in RTÉ's *Popstars* and won a place in the final band, Six, but could not take her place in the band. She had lied about her age, saying she was 18 when she was really just 16.

However, Coyle then entered the UK version of the show *Popstars: The Rivals* in 2002, where she began her career as a member of Girls Aloud. The band went on hiatus in 2009. Since then Coyle has released a solo album and is preparing another.

In 2007, Geoff Wray from Newbuildings impressed the judges of *The X Factor*. He made it through to the final fifty acts in the 'boot camp' stage. Sadly, Wray was found dead at his home in March 2012. His friends would later stage a thirty-six-hour drumming session in his honour to raise money for suicide prevention.

Dungiven teenager Eoghan Quigg auditioned for *The X Factor* in 2008 and made it to the final of the show, where he finished third. He released his first album the following year.

He narrowly missed out on representing Ireland in the 2014 Eurovision song contest, having finished second in an RTÉ contest to select the Irish entry.

In 2009, Gulladuff's Niamh McGlinchy entered *The All Ireland Talent Show* on RTÉ. She made it to the live finals but was voted out. Since then she has released an album titled *One Way Destination*.

In 2011, Damian McGinty won reality TV show *The Glee Project*. As a result, he appeared in sixteen episodes of the hit US show *Glee* as Rory Flanagan. He is also a member of Celtic Thunder.

Rachael O'Connor, from Drumsurn, auditioned for BBC's *The Voice* in 2014. She became part of Kylie Minogue's team. She made it through several rounds of the show, but was eventually eliminated in the quarter-final.

FESTIVALS

Glasgowbury

Glasgowbury began in 2000, with the aim of raising awareness for the Ulster Cancer Foundation. It was held in Draperstown annually until 2013 and hosted acts including Ash, The Answer and Henry McCullough. The event won lots of awards including a UK Promoter of the Year award for founder Paddy Glasgow at the 2013 UK Festival Awards.

City of Derry Jazz and Big Band Festival

This festival has gone from strength to strength since its launch in 2002. The annual festival brings jazz, blues, salsa and swing music to venues across the city each spring and has played host to big names like Jools Holland and Jamie Cullum.

Stendhal Festival of Art

Launched in 2011, this festival is held in the grounds of a farm outside Limavady. It has lots of gigs across several stages which have seen the likes of Duke Special and Neil Hannon of the Divine Comedy and 'My Lovely Horse' fame – who spent his early years in Derry city.

In addition to music the festival also offers art exhibitions and workshops, poetry and theatre and even morning yoga sessions. The event performs well at the Irish Festival Awards having won Best Small Festival two years in a row, as well as Best Line-up and the Family Festival Award.

BBC One Big Weekend

The BBC holds this festival in a different city or town within the UK each year. It first came to Derry in April 2004, when the likes of Faithless, Avril Lavigne, Judge Jules and Franz Ferdinand played to over 10,000 people at Prehen Playing Fields over two days.

In 2013, it was the first location to host the festival twice. The three-day event in May was held in Ebrington Square with a line-up full of big names, including Biffy Clyro, Rita Ora, Calvin Harris, Bruno Mars, Ellie Goulding and alt-J.

Ebrington Square was the site of big concerts yet again in 2014 when 20,000 people turned out for gigs from Professor Green, Afrojack and MNEK as part of MTV's Crashes concerts.

Fleadh Cheoil na hÉireann

The 2013 Fleadh in Derry was the first time the event had been held in Northern Ireland and with over 430,000 people flocking to the city, it was by far the biggest Fleadh in the event's more than sixty-year history.

The eight-day festival had performances and talks from many locals including Cara Dillon and Damien O'Kane as well as acts from across Ireland like Dervish and Patsy Dan Rogers, the King of Tory Island.

There were lots of other activities on offer including ceilidhs, art exhibitions and competitions in singing, whistling and a range of instruments from the tin whistle and bodhrán to the saxophone and piano.

The highlight of the festival was probably the merging of poetry and music in *The Poet and the Piper* with Seamus Heaney and uilleann piper Liam O'Flynn. The concert was held just two weeks before Heaney's death in August 2013.

WRITING

Cecil Frances Alexander

Cecil Frances Humphreys (1818-1895) moved to Strabane from Dublin at the age of 15. There she began to write poetry and hymns. When she was 30 she published a book, *Hymns for Little Children*, which contains some hymns that remain popular today including *All Things Bright and Beautiful* and *Once in Royal David's City*. Two years later she married Revd William Alexander, a Derry man.

She worked with the deaf in Derry and set up an institution to help with their education. The couple moved around but settled in the city in 1867, when William became Bishop of Derry and Raphoe. Cecil spent the rest of her life there and was buried in the City Cemetery.

William Alexander would go on to become the Archbishop of Armagh and took a seat in the House of Lords. A blue plaque in commemoration of Cecil Alexander can be found on her former home on Bishop Street.

James Burke

Derry city-born Burke became a household name in the United Kingdom as a presenter of the science series *Tomorrow's World*. He was also the commentator chosen by the BBC to cover the Apollo 11 moon landing in 1969.

He continues to write and make television shows about scientific subjects, particularly the history of technology and the influence computers may have on the future of humanity.

Nik Cohn

Although born in London in 1946, Cohn spent his childhood and adolescence in Derry. He wrote many articles for *The Guardian* and *The Observer* as a rock critic and has published several books.

His story about disco culture in New York, *Tribal Rites of the New Saturday Night*, was the inspiration for the 1977 hit film *Saturday Night Fever* starring John Travolta.

He has been extremely influential in the rock world. One of his novels from the 1960s is said to have inspired Davie Bowie's character Ziggy Stardust, while his love of pinball is said to have influenced Pete Townshend when he wrote The Who's famous song 'Pinball Wizard'.

Alan Davidson

Although born in Derry city, Davidson was schooled and went to university in England. He then travelled around the world with the British Navy and the Foreign Office. Always eager to uncover culinary secrets wherever he visited, he wrote several popular books on food and cookery.

His greatest work, the encyclopedic *Oxford Companion to Food*, took him twenty years to write. At over a million words, it is a formidable guide to all things edible. There are 2,650 alphabetical entries on the history of food, beginning with aardvark and ending with zuppa inglese, an Italian dessert.

He died in 2003 at the age of 79.

Seamus Deane

Deane attended St Columb's College where the city boy became friends with country lad Seamus Heaney. He has published several volumes of poetry but is best known for his first novel, *Reading in the Dark*.

The 1996 novel focuses on the life of a Catholic man from Derry city who witnessed the aftermath of Ireland's partition in the 1920s and the Troubles of the 1960s and 1970s. It won literary awards from *The Guardian* and *The Irish Times* and was shortlisted for the Booker Prize.

Brian Friel

Although born in Tyrone, the 'Irish Chekov' has always had close links to Derry. He attended St Columb's College and spent ten years as a mathematics teacher in the area. His most popular plays include *Philadelphia Here I Come!* and *Translations*, which premièred at the Guildhall in 1980, featuring Liam Neeson and the late Mick Lally.

His most famous play is probably *Dancing at Lughnasa,* which won both an Olivier Award and a Tony Award for Best Play. The play was adapted for the screen in 1998 with Meryl Streep, Michael Gambon and Kathy Burke in starring roles.

Friel also established the Field Day Theatre Company in Derry city with actor Stephen Rea. The company has put on world premieres of plays by local writers, including Derek Mahon, Tom Paulin and Seamus Heaney. Friel passed away in October 2015 at the age of 86.

George Farqhuar

The son of a clergyman in Derry city, Farqhuar (1677-1707) attended the Free School in Derry and later Trinity College, Dublin. It's not known exactly where he was or what he was doing during the siege, but an implausible suggestion has been made that the 13-year-old Farqhuar was somehow at the Battle of the Boyne in 1690.

He tried his hand at acting in Dublin, but during one performance he seriously wounded a fellow actor, as the sword he was using turned out to be no prop but instead was a real rapier. This incident caused him to leave acting behind and move to London to write comedic plays.

Although he wrote relatively few plays they were well received due to the eccentric rougish characters and engaging plots. He finished *The Beaux' Stratagem* on his deathbed and died a few weeks after it was first performed, aged just twenty-nine. Another well known work is *The Recruiting Officer.*

A blue plaque was erected in his memory in 2009. It can be found at the Verbal Arts Centre, believed to be close to where the Free School once was. Some attribute the phrase 'Necessity is the mother of invention' to Farqhuar; however, the origin of this phrase appears to be much older and appears in Plato's *Republic*.

Seamus Heaney

Born in 1939, Heaney was the eldest of nine children. He was raised and educated in Bellaghy before winning a scholarship to attend St Columb's College in Derry city. His brother Christopher (4) was killed in a road accident when Heaney was still at the school. One of his most famous poems 'Mid-Term Break' would reveal his feelings about this terrible event.

He went on to study English at Queen's University, Belfast, where he became friends with other prominent poets, like Michael Longley and Derek Mahon.

He published his first book of poetry, *Death of a Naturalist*, in 1966 and would publish a further eleven poetry collections in his lifetime. He also translated several important works like *Sweeney Astray* from the Irish, *The Cure at Troy* from Sophocles's Greek and *Beowulf*, which was originally written in Old English.

Heaney's work was always concerned with his native County Derry. The places and people that appear in his poems are both local and universal at the same time. He took our small

place and showed it to the world so that the quiet, decent voice of Derry's people could be heard over the disturbing commotion of sounds and images that many thought summed up Northern Ireland.

He was a much-needed beacon of peacefulness, humour and intelligence for the county and the country at a time of great violence.

He was awarded the Nobel Prize for Literature in 1995 and would receive many more major awards for his poetry. He taught at Queen's University, Harvard, the University of California at Berkeley (named for the former Bishop of Derry) and was appointed a professor of poetry at Oxford.

He died in Dublin in August 2013 at the age of 74. He is buried in Bellaghy, not far from the grave of his brother Christopher.

In 2004, Queen's opened the Seamus Heaney Centre for Poetry in the poet's honour. The teaching staff includes some of Ireland's greatest living poets, like Medbh McGuckian, Ciaran Carson and Sinead Morrissey. Carson and Morrissey have followed in Heaney's footsteps by winning the prestigious T.S. Eliot Prize.

Eamonn McCann

Born and raised in Derry city, McCann was a pupil at St Columb's before studying at Queen's University, Belfast. McCann, a gifted political speaker, was president of the University's Debating Society.

McCann was a prominent figure in the Civil Rights movement in Derry in the 1960s. He was one of the founders of the Derry Housing Action Committee (DHAC) and worked with Bernadette Devlin in her campaign to be elected MP for Mid-Ulster.

Following the Troubles he worked as a journalist and became involved with socialist politics. He is a member of the Socialist Worker's Party and has stood for election several times with the Socialist Environmental Alliance and the People Before Profit Alliance. He finally became an MLA for People Before Profit in May 2016 at the age of 73 but would later lose his seat during the January 2017 Assembly Election

He has also forged a reputation as an activist with a sharp mind, always ready to bring politicians north and south of the border down a peg or two with a cutting remark. He continues to work as a journalist, with columns in the *Derry Journal*, *The Irish Times* and *Hot Press* magazine.

Nell McCafferty

A journalist from the Bogside, McCafferty has established herself as a social commentator and fierce enemy of what she perceives as homophobic or hypocritical elements in the Irish Church and State.

In 1971, McCafferty led forty-nine members of The Irish Women's Liberation Movement from Dublin to Belfast. The trip on what became known as 'the contraceptive train' was in protest against the fact that contraceptives were illegal in the Republic. The women were unable to buy the pill, needing a prescription, so brought aspirin tablets home instead (as they looked similar) and then publicly swallowed these 'contraceptive' pills to show their contempt for the restrictions.

She had a relationship with novelist Nuala O'Faolain for over fifteen years. She spoke about her relationship with O'Faolian and the difficulties of growing up gay in Ireland in her 2004 autobiography, *Nell*.

Brian McGilloway

An English teacher at St Columb's College, Gilloway has written five crime novels to date, featuring detectives Benedict Devlin (named after his first son) and Lucy Black. His fifth novel, *Little Girl Lost*, was a number one bestseller in the United Kingdom and was also a *New York Times* Bestseller.

After winning the Tony Doyle Award for a screenplay in 2014, McGilloway became writer-in-residence with BBC Northern Ireland.

James Simmons

A polymath from Derry city, Simmons was a poet, literary critic, songwriter and teacher.

His most enduring legacy is the founding of the literary magazine the *Honest Ulsterman* in 1968, which gave many greats their start in poetry, including Ciaran Carson, Paul Muldoon and Stevie Smith. He died in 2001 at the age of 68.

ACTING

Amanda Burton

Burton left her native Derry city for England when she was 18 and has since became a familiar face on British television. She has appeared in *Waterloo Road*, *Peak Practice* and *Brookside*, but her most famous role is undoubtedly her portrayal of forensic pathologist Sam Ryan in the BBC series *Silent Witness*.

Roma Downey

Downey was raised in the Bogside and began acting while a pupil at Thornhill College. She met and married a classmate while studying in England and the pair moved to New York. Although the marriage did not work out, Downey's career took off in America with roles in Broadway shows and parts on television.

Her role as Monica in *Touched by an Angel* earned her both Emmy and Golden Globe nominations, while her portrayal of Mary in the television series *The Bible* brought her to the attention of a massive audience of over 100 million in the United States alone.

She also appeared in the music video for 'Mary, Did You Know?' with Cee-Lo Green of Gnarls Barkley.

Bronagh Gallagher

Born and raised in Derry city, Gallagher first found fame playing Bernie in the 1991 film *The Commitments*. Roles in Hollywood soon followed including *Pulp Fiction*, *Sherlock Holmes* and *Star Wars: The Phantom Menace*.

She also pursued a career in music and has released two albums to date. In addition to singing and songwriting she also played the drums for songs on her albums.

Michelle Fairley

Fairley was born and raised in Coleraine. She honed her skills as an actress throughout the 1980s and '90s, working both in theatre and on television.

Her biggest roles came in 2010, when she appeared as Hermione Granger's mother in *Harry Potter and the Deathly Hallows*, which was soon followed by a part in *Game of Thrones*.

Her portrayal of Catelyn Stark in the HBO fantasy series led to other roles in popular American shows including *Suits*, *24* and *Resurrection*.

Jimeoin

Born James Eoin McKeown in Portstewart, Jimeoin believes that his unusual nickname was an invention by his mother. He moved to Australia where he became a household name following an eponymous television series that ran for three seasons.

He has also appeared in several films and on television in the United Kingdom, particularly on *8 Out of 10 Cats* and *Live at the Apollo*.

James Nesbitt

Although he was born in Ballymena, County Antrim, Nesbitt's family moved to Coleraine when he was 11. He attended Coleraine Academical Institution and took up acting at the nearby Riverside

Theatre. He started a degree in French at the University of Ulster, Jordanstown, but left after a year to move to London.

He got his big break in 1998 as Adam Williams in *Cold Feet*. Since then he has appeared in many prominent films including *Bloody Sunday*, *Five Minutes of Heaven* (alongside Liam Neeson), *Waking Ned* and most recently as the dwarf Bofur in Peter Jackson's *The Hobbit* trilogy.

In 2010, he was appointed as the Chancellor of the University of Ulster.

Laura Pyper

Pyper, a native of Magherafelt, landed her first big acting role while studying at Trinity College Dublin. She appeared in *Reign of Fire* alongside Matthew McConaughey and Christian Bale and continued to appear in supernatural programmes as a regular on the Sky One show *Hex*, which starred Michael Fassbender. She also was the voice of Lexine Murdoch in the horror game for the Wii and Playstation 3, *Dead Space: Extraction*.

She has had roles in *Holby City*, *Luther* and *The IT Crowd*, where she appeared alongside her former boyfriend Chris O'Dowd.

Andrew Simpson

Simpson was only a teenager when he appeared in his first films. First he played a pupil at a reformatory school in the 2003 *Song for a Raggy Boy*, alongside Aidan Quinn and Iain Glen.

His big break came when he was 18 and still studying at Foyle College. He played a schoolboy who has an affair with his school teacher, played by Cate Blanchett, in *Notes on a Scandal* which was nominated for four Oscars.

Noel Willman

Willman began acting at Foyle College in the 1930s before moving to London to work in the theatre. He moved onto the silver screen, appearing in several Hammer horror films. He worked alongside James Stewart and Doris Day in *The Man Who Knew Too Much* and played Razin beside Omar Sharif in *Doctor Zhivago*.

He died on Christmas Eve 1988, after suffering a heart attack while in a New York cinema.

Jayne Wisener

Wisener was plucked from obscurity aged just nineteen, when she won a role in the film *Sweeney Todd* directed by Tim Burton and starring Johnny Depp.

The Coleraine actress has since appeared in *Misfits* and *The Inbetweeners*. She also appeared in *The Life and Adventures of Nick Nickleby* on BBC Television, featuring fellow Derry actors Bronagh Gallagher and Andrew Simpson.

VISUAL ARTS

Willie Carson

After passing through several roles at the *Derry Journal*, Carson struck out on his own as a freelance photo-journalist in 1968. Many of the images that appeared around the world during the Troubles were ones that Carson had taken. One of his images was nominated for the prestigious Pulitzer Prize in 1972.

In 2007 the Guildhall Press reprinted his 1976 collection *Derry Through the Lens: Refocus* in response to public demand.

Willie Doherty

Artist Doherty has kept his hometown of Derry city as a central element in his work. He mainly works in the mediums of photography and video – many of which feature a voice-over by the artist.

His work has been displayed in prominent art galleries around the world, including the Museum of Modern Art (MOMA) in New York, London's Tate Gallery and De Appel, Amsterdam. He has been nominated for the Turner Prize twice, in 1994 and 2003.

Maurice Harron

A native of Derry city, Harron has worked as a teacher in both St Columb's College and Lumen Christi College. He began to produce sculptures in the 1980s and has since created some of the most recognisable works in Ulster. These include *Let the Dance Begin*, featuring five musicians and dancers made from steel and bronze, which stand near the Lifford Bridge in Strabane.

His sculpture *Reconciliation-Hands Across the Divide*, located near the Craigavon Bridge in Derry, is an instantly recognisable icon for the city.

Éamonn O'Doherty

Derry city-born O'Doherty is the man behind some of the most famous public sculptures in Ireland. His works include the *Quincentennial Sculpture* in Eyre Square, Galway, as well as the *James Connolly*

Memorial and the *Anna Livia Monument* – affectionately called the 'floozie in the jacuzzi' – which are both in Dublin.

He held various teaching positions around the world. He died in August 2011 following a long battle with throat cancer, aged seventy-two. An exhibition of his work was held in Derry in 2013, including the sculpture known as the *Armoured Pram for Derry*, which was designed to look like a tank.

Hugh Thomson

Raised in Coleraine and Kilrea, Thomson would become an illustrator renowned for his attention to detail. His is considered to be one of the finest illustrators of the Victorian age, due to his work with Macmillan & Co, which included illustrating the work of Jane Austen, Charles Dickens and George Eliot.

In 2007, Coleraine Council bought more than 500 examples of Thomson's art. A collection of his works has since been exhibited in Coleraine Town Hall and in Derry's Tower Museum.

Turner Prize

In 2013 the Turner Prize was held at Ebrington Barracks. This was the first time that the prize had been held outside of England. Thousands of people visited the exhibitions from October to January 2014 to consider the work of the four nominees. In the end, the Prize was awarded to Laure Prouvost for her video installations, *Wantee* and *Grandma's Dream*.

Comics and Animation

Dave McElfatrick, a native of Coleraine, found fame with the web comic *Cyanide and Happiness*. More than 130,000 fans of the cartoons signed a petition to allow McElfatrick to join the other writers of the comic in the United States. The cartoons feature stick figures in extremely controversial situations, which have earned the writers an audience of millions.

Puffin Rock

Derry-based company Dog Ears has recently created an animated series about a family of puffins. The firm joined up with publisher Penguin and Irish animation studio Cartoon Saloon, which has been nominated for an Oscar, to create *Puffin Rock*.

Half of the animation was created in the Derry office, while the team at Dog Ears also took care of the scripting and voices for the show.

The first episode of the show aired in January 2015, on RTÉ Jr in Ireland and Nick Jr in the United Kingdom. The show features the voice talent of Chris O'Dowd, star of *The IT Crowd* and *Bridemaids*. A range of books connected with the programme will be published by Penguin in the near future.

Derry Girls

Derry Girls premieres on Channel 4 in January 2018. It follows the exploits of teenage girls Erin, Orla, Clare and Michelle as they grow up in 1990s Derry city. The series has been praised widely by viewers and critics alike. It boasts fans around the world thanks to streaming service Netflix, while the Maiden City expressed their love for the show by unveiling a mural featuring the main characters in the city centre.

6

MYTHS, LEGENDS AND TALL TALES

It is no accident that Derry has produced world-class story tellers, like Seamus Heaney, as the county is not short of a few fellas fond of a tall tale. Drop into a pub anywhere in Derry and nine times out of ten, you'll run into that one 'auld fella' that claims to have fought Muhammad Ali (and won!) or that he held a bucket for Robert De Niro, who spent his youth washing windows in Kilrea.

Here is a selection of the most peculiar of these stories. By the end of the chapter you may never look at the county the same way again, as you are shown the monsters, magic and mysteries of Derry.

ST COLUMBA-COLMCILLE AND THE LOCH NESS MONSTER

Derry's patron saint is believed to have been born around 521, near Loch Gartan in what is now County Donegal. His family are said to have been members of the O'Neill clan and descendants of Niall of the Nine Hostages.

He was originally baptised as Criomhthann, meaning fox; however, he soon acquired the nickname Colum, meaning dove, which would lead to Colm Cille or 'the dove of the church'.

He is said to have founded a monastery in Derry. Aodh mac Ainmhireach, the High King of Ireland, had a house that he donated to Columba. The saint burnt this house to the ground, very nearly setting fire to a nearby forest in the process. He explained to the king that he wanted to make a fresh start and set about constructing a church out of wood. A community grew around the church known as 'The Oak-trees of Colum Cille' or 'Doire Colum Cille'.

He is described as being a rather imposing figure who was powerfully built and not averse to violence. A dispute arose when he made a copy of a psalter (book of psalms) belonging to St Finnian of Dromin, County Louth, without permission. The two saints brought their case to the High King who judged that Columba was in the wrong, saying 'To every cow its calf, to every book its copy'. This statement has been taken as perhaps the earliest example of a copyright law in recorded history.

Columba, hot-head that he was, did not take the ruling well, going so far as to warn the king that he would pay for his unfair judgement. Following a rash decision by the High King where he executed a son of the King of Connacht, Columba raised a force of men and a battle between the two sides took place in Sligo. Some 3,000 warriors died in the Battle of Cúl Dreimne (Battle of the Book) and the victorious Columba left the battlefield with his book, having defeated the High King of Ireland.

The book became known as the Cathach (Battle-book) and became a good luck charm for the clan of Conall, of which Columba was a member.

There is a psalter preserved to this day in the Royal Irish Academy in Dublin, which may be the very book Columba deemed so precious.

As penance for such violence, fellow saints excommunicated Columba and he was sent into exile. He travelled to Scotland and landed on the small island of Iona, where he founded a monastery. Saints, scholars and kings would come to the island, seeking his advice, though he also had time for the common man. In one tale, Columba was called upon by a young farmer to drive out a demon that had taken up residence in his bucket of milk!

The most interesting episode in Columba's life was his encounter with the Loch Ness Monster. The story is believed to be the first documented account of the 'beastie'.

While travelling in the area near Loch Ness, he heard of many deaths caused by a monster in the water. Columba ordered one of his followers to go for a swim in the loch. The monster is then said to have darted after the man, with terrible jaws and a deafening roar.

But Columba simply raised his hand, said 'Thou shalt go no further, nor touch the man' and the monster fled in terror. Columba must have made a strong impression because Nessie has been in hiding ever since ...

Columba lived on Iona into his seventies and died in AD 597. It is said that at the time of his death fishermen in Donegal witnessed the night sky turning a bright as day and saw a 'huge column of fire' rising from the earth to heaven. On Columba's feast day, 9 June, many people in Derry wear oak leaves on their lapels.

A CARD GAME

One of Derry city's most unnerving stories may have taken place in a blacksmith's forge at the top of Howard Street. A group of men would meet in the forge and pass the time playing cards. None of them were particularly wealthy so the game was more for fun than the chance to win much money.

One of the regulars met a stranger in a pub and brought him along to the card game one night. The others reluctantly let the stranger join the game, but soon found themselves warming to him when he began losing large sums of cash! The men grew excited and began betting a lot, well beyond their means in fact, in the hope of taking the newcomer for all he was worth.

But the man's luck began to turn and he was soon on a winning streak. The stakes grew higher and the card players tried to win their money back. One man became so frustrated that he said he would sell his soul just to beat the stranger.

The mood darkened then. The stranger laughed and thumped the table, scattering cards and coins all over the floor. The dealer bent to pick up the cards and was horrified to see the stranger's feet. He had cloven hooves. The dealer took off running, shouting to the other card players to do the same.

However, the man who said he would sell his soul found himself frozen to the spot. Two men returned to save him and had to wrestle their friend from the powerful grip of the stranger. They managed to free him and run away, but could see the imprint of fingers burnt into the man's arm. The forge burst into flames behind them and had burnt to the ground completely by morning.

MAGIC AND WELLS

It is said that there is an ancient holy well in Moneyneany, which was under the protection of a magician called Sir Volvett. He wanted to prevent others from using the well, so he chained an earless dog to it, which is why the well became known as Toberawathymeel or 'the earless dog's well'.

Apparently it was not so unusual to be a magician in the area, as Moneyneany was a favourite place for warriors to practise and perform magic. This is where the name Moneyneany comes from, which means 'the bog of wonders'.

Speaking of wells, there are tales of the healing properties of St Ringan's Well at Bovevagh Old Church. People would bring delicate children to the well to be dipped in the water and it is believed that the sight of a blind boy was restored by visiting the well. A farmer learned of this and hoped to improve his fortunes by restoring the sight of his blind horse. He washed the horse's eyes with water from the well and the horse's sight was restored. Yet the farmer lost his own sight and the well dried up soon after.

SAINTS AND SERPENTS

In a small pool in a quiet part of Banagher Forest near Feeny, an enormous serpent is said to sleep, curled up. The legend goes that when St Patrick was busy driving all of the snakes out of Ireland, he overlooked this one, named Lig-na-paiste.

It was described as a terrible creature like a dragon that could breathe fire, had potent venom and the horns of a ram. It ravaged the local countryside so terribly that the locals turned to holy man St Murrough O'Heaney in desperation.

Confronting the serpent, he managed to put three bands of rushes on it, which then transformed into bands of iron, trapping the serpent and making it sink under the water. Some attribute unusual currents on the north County Derry coast to Lig-na-Paiste writhing around, trying to escape its bonds.

St Murrough is also said to have founded Banagher Old Church, when a stag carrying a book on its antlers led him to the site. His remains are believed to lie in a mortuary house in the churchyard. Locals believe that sand taken from this grave brings good luck, particularly when scattered over a horse preparing for a race.

THE DRUMCEATT CONVENTION

In AD 575 a convention was called by Ireland's High King, Aedh, so that nobles, chiefs and scholars could discuss the Kingdom of Dal Riata, which contained territory in both Ireland and Scotland. Eventually, it was agreed that the Irish would pay allegiance to the Scottish King, Aedán, but would also come to the aid of Ireland in times of war.

The convention was held at Mullagh Hill, which is now part of the golf course at the Roe Park Resort. Another matter for discussion was the powerful influence of bards (storytellers and poets) in Ireland. Some people at the time felt that bards made too many demands and should be banned.

The bards called upon St Columba to champion their cause and he returned from his exile to Scotland to preside over the event. When he left he swore he would never see Ireland, or set foot on its soil, again. Legend has it that when he returned he was blindfolded and had sods of Scottish earth tied to his feet to avoid breaking his vow.

The saint managed to work out a compromise, enabling bards to remain in Ireland, although with much less influence and in far fewer numbers.

ABHARTACH THE VAMPIRE

In the fifth century, parts of County Derry were ruled by chieftains, including the O'Cahans in Dungiven and an 'evil tyrant' called Abhartach around Glenullin.

He was described as being a powerful wizard and some sources also suggest that he may have been a dwarf. The locals were scared of Abhartach and appealed to the chieftain of the O'Cahans to get rid of him. After some persuasion, the chieftain killed him and buried him standing up. But the next day Abhartach was back.

The tyrant had risen from the dead and demanded a bowl of blood from each of his subjects. O'Cahan arrived and killed him again, only for him to return again the following day.

And on it went back and forth. Most people who are killed three times in a row by the same person might considering avoiding fights with that person, or perhaps running and hiding. Abhartach might have been an evil, undead, blood-drinking tyrant, but he was certainly not the wisest.

When O'Cahan's arm eventually got tired, he spoke to a local saint who said that Abhartach, a 'Dearg-Dul', could not be killed permanently but could be prevented from returning from the dead by following a very specific ritual. He had to be stabbed with a stake made from yew, buried upside down with thorns around the grave and a big stone, called a leacht, on top for good measure. His burial site gives the area its name – Slaughtaverty, meaning Abhartach's leacht.

The legend became widely known across Ireland. Some believe it may have reached the ears of Dublin-born author Bram Stoker and that he was so inspired by the Derry vampire that he turned him into a Count from Transylvania in his famous Gothic novel, *Dracula*.

CLOSE ENCOUNTERS

In 2010 there were several sightings of flying red objects in the sky near Derry city. Two eyewitnesses reported seeing a silent, bright red object that could move extremely quickly and 'looked like a stealth bomber'. A week after these sightings, an anonymous Derry man said that he saw a 'bright orange light followed by a small white dot' in the sky over Bishop Street. He said that it didn't move at all like a plane and was extremely fast.

Yet another sighting was reported of six to ten bright orange balls above the city which were 'like flames burning with a tail behind them'. Armagh Planetarium suggested that they may have been meteors, as they recorded some activity over the city that night. This was challenged by another eyewitness who said the lights they saw were moving much too slowly to be meteors.

Many believe that the witnesses were simply mistaking Chinese lanterns, usually released at weddings, for intergalactic aircraft. However, UFO expert Betty Meyler claims that aliens may be attracted to the area by the substantial 'energy' generated from ancient structures such as megalithic sites near the city.

There are also reported UFO sightings from areas across the county. The strangest tale may the report of an encounter near Magherafelt in April 1998. A group of people were walking in a wooded area when they noticed a light in a sky. The person reporting the sighting said they saw a ship in the sky that 'changed from an oval shape to a disc shape' and following a flash of light they woke up on a cold bench onboard the spacecraft.

They said that they were operated on by beings with oval-shaped heads and claim to have the scars as proof of the encounter. After this the group were returned to the spot that they had been – but arrived three hours before they had initially left.

THE LEAPING DOG OF LIMAVADY

The O'Cahans ruled the Roe Valley area for centuries from castles in both Dungiven and Limavady. They were often at war with the neighbouring clans and on one occasion, their Limavady castle was under siege from an enemy clan.

Legend has it that the O'Cahans sent a dog to signal reinforcements from Dungiven. The dog leaped over the River Roe, alerted the warriors and saved the day. The spot from where it jumped is still referred to as the 'Dogleap' today and the town takes its name from the story. Limavady is the anglicised version of Léim an Mhadaidh, Irish for 'leap of the dog'.

Near to the Dogleap, in the Roe Valley Country Park, is O'Cahan's Rock, the site of a similar legend. In this tale a member of the O'Cahan clan is said to have escaped his pursuers by having his horse also leap straight across the river. It is said that you can still make out the horse's hoof print on the rock.

Before going to the Country Park for an evening of river leaping, in the interest of health and safety it is worth pointing out that leaping off O'Cahan's Rock – an eighty-foot drop into cold water – is more likely to land you in a hospital bed rather than the history books.

Still, while enjoying the Roe Valley Country Park, visitors have the chance to see where the 2014 film *Dracula Untold* was filmed. What remains of O'Cahan's castle can also be seen. It was demolished in the seventeenth century by an English solider named Sir Thomas Philips. Philips founded 'Newtownlimavady' in 1613 and built a water mill on the River Roe.

THE GEM OF THE ROE

Another legend concerning the River Roe is that of Finvola O'Cahan. She was considered to be the 'Gem' of the Roe Valley due to her beauty. A Scottish chief visiting the area fell in love with her and they married. Finvola's father, an O'Cahan's chieftain called Dermot, agreed to the marriage on the condition that Finvola be buried in Dungiven when she died.

Finvola died soon after reaching her husband's homeland on the island of Islay. However, in his grief, her husband could not bear to send her home and buried her on the island.

Soon afterwards, Finvola's brothers heard terrible wailing coming from Benbradagh mountain. They recognised it as the call of Grainne Rua, the banshee of the O'Cahan clan. As the banshee calls only when a member of the family has died, and finding everyone in good health at home, the brothers travelled to Islay, recovered Finvola's body and stopped the wailing of the banshee.

THE SLIEVE
GALLION GIANT

When St Patrick was building his cathedral in Armagh he was terrorised by a monstrous black bull that would ruin any progress made on the construction at the end of each day.

Frustrated, Patrick thought he might have to abandon the cathedral, but was then told about a 'man of courage' named Teag More and sent for him.

Teag More lived at the foot of Slieve Gallion, a mountain at the very eastern edge of the Sperrins, about eight miles from Magherafelt. When he arrived in Armagh, he was blessed by St Patrick, and received enormous strength.

Teag was left to guard the area. When the bull arrived that evening, Teag seized an ash tree in one hand, grabbed the bull's tail in the other and began to give it a sound beating. The bull then ran off 'over the Blackwater and the Bann' and onwards to the top of Slieve Gallion, where it fell into a bog hole and was finally slain by Teag.

Quite an audience had gathered to watch the chase and the people were horrified when Teag, exhausted and hungry from the fight, began to devour the bull. The crowd prayed to St Patrick to take away Teag's fearsome new strength. But when Patrick took away his power, the strength of Teag's stomach failed and he died instantly. He was buried on the mountain in a place known as the giant's grave.

THE DEMON HUNTER

The story of St Ambrose O'Coffey is perhaps the first reference to an exorcist in Ireland. He is said to have been a preacher with powerful magical abilities who fought and killed demons.

He died in Magilligan in 1187, at a place called St Columcille's Seat. He was said to have left behind the 'Druid Library', a series of ancient manuscripts and scrolls detailing the ins and outs of exorcism and certain magic spells. It was believed to be one of the greatest collections of texts relating to witchcraft in Europe and rumour has it that some volumes were bound in tree bark and even human skin!

They were kept at a monastery in Duncrun, near Magilligan, until it was destroyed in 1203. The books were then supposedly spirited away and hidden so that they would not fall into the wrong hands.

However, another tale states that some of the texts were placed in 'St Columcille's Chest', itself a magical item which could only be opened by a man 'who had never been born who approached it on a horse that had never been born',

Luckily, the Earl Bishop Frederick Hervey was born 'unnaturally' by Caesarean section and knew where he could find a horse that had had a similar start in life. So when the chest was found during the construction of Mussenden Temple, he was able to open it and take a look at the Druid Library.

He was greatly disturbed by what he saw there, which was sadly never revealed and he instructed the chest be taken away to Derry. There is no mention of the Druid Library after that and no one knows what became of the powerful books on sorcery and the terrible, ancient knowledge they are said to contain.

TWO LOCAL SAINTS

Believed to have born near Limavady in AD 516, Canice (or Cainnech) was a great friend of Colmcille. He also travelled to Scotland, but returned to found monasteries in Kilkenny city and at Aghaboe, County Laois.

When he died, the men of the two monasteries are said to have fought over who had the right to bury him. While they fought however, a second coffin appeared. This settled the issue and both groups lifted a coffin to take home and bury. Yet, it is said that Aghaboe monastery declined soon afterwards, leading some to suggest that the saint is really buried in Kilkenny.

Kilkenny is named after him. In Irish the county and city are called 'Cill Chainnigh' meaning 'Church of Cainnech'. He is also the patron saint of Limavady and Dungiven, which is seen in the prominent use of his name in those areas.

St Aidan also left Ireland to become a missionary. When he died in AD 667, his successor Colman was bringing his remains back to Ireland and set out for Mayo. However, he lost his way and ended up in Magilligan. Taking the detour as a sign from God, he buried Aidan's bones there.

Colman also blessed a well in Magilligan. This well can still be visited today and the water is said to cure illnesses if mixed with dust from Aidan's burial site and applied to the afflicted area.

FAIRIES

Census records from the 1830s say that several people living in the Dungiven and Magilligan area reported being hit by objects thrown from passing 'fairy clouds'.

One old Dungiven lady showed the census investigator a purple bruise on her leg. She said that she had been drawing water from a well, when all of a sudden a strong wind blew up and she was hit by a 'fairy bolt' from a cloud. These fairy or elf bolts were said to be small hard objects like stones, which fairies, particularly those known as 'sluaghs', would throw at people and animals. She believed that she had been attacked as the fairies had taken exception at her use of the well.

The woman's daughter had a similar injury on her arm. She said that the fairies had been firing bolts for fun at the cattle she was tending, a practice that local farmers claim had killed sheep and cattle in the past.

Another story of fairies near Dungiven is altogether more tragic. A weaver named Joseph McPhearson was tormented by fairies in the late nineteenth century. They are said to have wrecked his house and kept him awake during the night. When his attempts to get rid of them with the help of religious men failed, McPhearson made a deal with the fairies. They would leave him in peace in exchange for the life of his next born child.

McPhearson and his wife felt they were past the age of having children so were unconcerned. However, his wife eventually did have a child, which the fairies took from them and killed. The heartbroken couple emigrated to America soon afterwards and never returned.

THE ARTICLAVE POLTERGEIST

One evening near Christmas in 1934, a family had no sooner gone to bed when strange and unnatural things began to happen.

A young girl, ten years old, was flung out of bed by an unseen force several times. She said that she felt as if she had been nipped and bitten or jagged with hot needles, a sensation that left red welts on her skin.

The spirit was soon making mischief around the house too. Objects would move around rooms, seemingly on their own and knocking sounds were heard in the dead of night. The father reported a tin of paint flying across the kitchen 'like a bullet', just missing his head. He also said that clothes were found to have been slashed, as if with a knife. The mother was knitting one evening and placed her work down for a second, but next thing she knew it was on the fire.

It was believed that this paranormal activity was due to the fact that the farmhouse where they lived had been built on the site of an ancient Celtic fort or rath. The family asked that a minister be brought in to exorcise the house but this was not successful.

The story spread and soon *The Irish Times* sent one of their journalists, J.P. Donaghy, up north from Dublin to investigate. In his reports the family is never identified and the girl's name is given as 'Laura', yet other reports identify the girl as Jeanie Ross, who lived in Articlave with her father David, her mother and two brothers.

As if in a Gothic novel, Donaghy arrived at the farmhouse just as a storm was gathering. The kitchen where he was welcomed, he said, was lit by a single oil lamp which cast ominous shadows on the wall.

Neighbours arrived as he is settling in, as they volunteered to take turns staying with the family. They talked into the wee hours until everyone, including the family's dog, dozed off. Donaghy says that at some point in the night, he imagined or dreamed that the kitchen door opened slightly, as if someone was peeping inside.

Around five o'clock in the morning a noise from the stairs woke Donaghy and the others. He followed members of the family as they went upstairs to Laura's room. The girl was in bed, terrified. She tried to speak but could not make a sound. Strange knocking sounds began to echo across the room. Donaghy investigated but could not find their source as they seemed to be coming from different places around the room.

A Church elder who was present began to ask the spirit questions, indicating that it should answer by knocking once for no and twice for yes. It responded accurately to questions that few could have possibly known, including correctly identifying the journalist's birthday from a list of dates. However, it refused to answer any questions about itself. Just before daylight the knocking stopped and Laura fell into a deep sleep.

Donaghy left and it is reported that the occurrences stopped soon afterwards. Laura continued to live in Articlave until her death and the house was eventually demolished.

Some believe that the strange events were caused by the unusual atmospheric conditions brought on by the storm or that the whole thing was an elaborate hoax. There is a rumour that the family had found themselves in financial turmoil and may have had to sell their home. This would have meant that the farm would likely fall out of Presbyterian hands into those of another faith, an issue that still concerns some people when selling their home or land today.

The 'ghost' in this interpretation then was merely a ruse to scare off anyone interested in buying the farm, orchestrated not only by the family, but also by members of the local church.

FAMILY AFFAIRS

St George Ashe was Bishop of Derry for the final year of his life, 1717. He was also a close friend of satirist Jonathan Swift, author of *Gulliver's Travels*. He is rumoured to have performed a secret marriage for Swift and Esther 'Stella' Johnson. Whether this really occurred is a topic still hotly debated by Swift scholars and it seems that the truth may never be fully known.

Henry Clarke, originally from Maghera, was a businessman and politician in New South Wales, Australia. He and his wife had eleven children, which seems like a lot, but on his eightieth birthday Clarke claimed to have 200 grandchildren and two great-grandchildren! That means that each of Clarke's children had to have had eighteen children of their own.

7

SPORT IN DERRY

Derry has developed a reputation for its sportspeople. Up and down the county there are clubs that perform well locally and nationally in a range of different sports.

Derry is no stranger to the world stage of sport too, as competitors flock to events like the Milk Cup and North West 200 to prove themselves. There are also numerous Olympic medallists and world champions who first learned their trade on Derry's pitches, roads and rivers.

GAA

Derry has forty GAA clubs, thirty-two of which are Gaelic football, two are hurling and six are both sports.

Football

Derry is overwhelmingly a Gaelic football county. The county team has won the All-Ireland Championship only once, in 1993, although they reached the final in 1958 and have won the National League six times.

As for clubs, Bellaghy became All-Ireland club football champions in 1972, beating Cork's University College Cork (UCC) 0-15 to 1-11.

Lavey followed and beat Salthill, County Galway well on St Patrick's Day 1991, with a final score of Lavey 2-9 to Salthill's 0-10.

Balinderry were the next Derry football club to go all the way. They faced Nemo Rangers of Cork in Semple Stadium in Tipperary in 2002. They overcame the Rangers, All-Ireland winners six times in the past, scoring 2-10 to the Corkmen's 0-9.

Slaughtneil had a very disappointing campaign when they lost 0-7 to Corofin, County Clare, who scored 1-14 to take the 2015 All-Ireland club title. Slaughtneil reached the final again in 2017, but unfortunately missed out on the title again. They were defeated by two points (1–9 to 1–7) by Kerry based club Dr Crokes.

Two Derry teams also took part in RTÉ's television show *Celebrity Bainisteoir*, which saw celebrities take charge of football clubs and go head-to-head in a tournament.

The first series in 2008 saw Derry city's Nell McCafferty, a journalist and playwright, manage St Mary's, Faughanvale. The team beat Galtee Gaels from County Limerick to reach the semi-final, but were then knocked out of the contest by Whelan's Maryland, from County Westmeath. Maryland would go on to win the competition.

Lissan also featured in series four of the programme, in 2011. They were initially managed by the singer Dana. However, she withdrew from the contest to focus on her Irish Presidential campaign.

Majella O'Donnell, the wife of the Donegal singer Daniel O'Donnell, then stepped in to manage the team. Like St Mary's, Lissan made it to the semi-final of the contest but were then defeated by Oughterard, County Galway. O'Donnell took the team out for a drink in Galway city after the game, but the occasion was marred when a 'pub brawl' broke out. Two Lissan players later appeared in court and managed to escape conviction, by agreeing to make a donation of €300 to the court's poor box.

Ladies football began in the county in the 1990s, when the men's senior team were performing well. There are currently nineteen clubs in the county.

Hurling

Derry's hurlers cannot hope to imitate the success of their counterparts in football, but they hold their own. They defeated Cavan 2-8 to 0-2 to claim the 1908 Ulster Senior Hurling final, but had to wait over ninety years to regain the title. Their next win came at long last in 2000 when they edged out Antrim by only one point. The score was 0-19 for Antrim to Derry's 4-8.

Once they had broken the curse, they managed to keep the magic alive by defending their title against Down the following year. Derry were victorious by a single point yet again, scoring 1-17 to Down's 3-10. The 2001 victory was only Derry's fourth Ulster Hurling Championship title in their history, which is impressive considering that Antrim completely dominate the sport in Ulster, having won fifty-four Ulster titles and that Cavan and Armagh have yet to win the championship.

Camogie

There is also an active Camogie scene in County Derry. Several of the clubs have been active for more than eighty years. The county team perform well in Ulster and several of the women have won All Star awards for their performance.

Slaughtneil's camogie team has emerged in recent years to dominate the club scene. The team won their first All-Ireland in 2017, beating Galway side Sarfields 1–10 to 11 points. The two sides met again in 2018 with Slaughtneil dominating Sarfields even more scoring 2–11 to their 1–9. In March 2019 Slaughtneil lifted the All-Ireland title for the third year in a row, having overcome St Martin's of Wexford with a score of 1–9 to 0–7.

Joe Brolly

Dungiven man Joe Brolly was a corner forward for Derry's football team throughout their run of success in the 1990s. While he was a member of the team, the county won two Ulster Championships, four National League titles and an All Ireland title. For his efforts as an individual, Brolly was awarded two All Star awards, in 1996 and in 1997.

Brolly is a barrister and has been involved in several high-profile cases involving alleged members of Republican paramilitary groups.

He is perhaps best known today for being a vocal and controversial GAA commentator, a role that has landed him in hot water on many occasions.

In 2012, Brolly donated one of his own kidneys to his friend Shane Finnegan, who had been waiting for over six years for a transplant. Unfortunately the transplant failed soon afterwards and the kidney had to be removed. Following this Brolly has been an outspoken advocate of an opt-out system for organ donation and has devoted a great deal of time to raising awareness of the current and proposed laws around organ donation.

FOOTBALL

The Candystripes

Derry City FC are the only football team from Northern Ireland competing in the League of Ireland and one of only two Ulster teams, the other being their rivals Finn Harps from Ballybofey, County Donegal.

The team was founded in 1928, taking over from two teams that had previously represented the city – Derry Celtic and Derry Olympic. The club first entered competition in the Irish League, a tournament for teams from Northern Ireland. The team won the Irish Cup twice in the 1930s and later topped the League in 1965.

Tensions rose at the club's matches as violence often broke out in the city during the late 1960s and early 1970s. As their stadium, the Brandywell, was close to the Bogside, the Royal Ulster Constabulary (RUC) decided it was not suitable for fixtures. The team were then forced to travel to Coleraine to play their 'home' games, which many fans resented. When the team attempted to return to the Brandywell this was prevented, following a vote by Irish League members. As a result, Derry City looked to the south for competition.

Derry joined teams from the Republic of Ireland in the League of Ireland in 1985, with the Brandywell restored as their home ground. Since entering the League, Derry have won the Premier League twice, in 1988 and 1996, although they have been runners-up on three other occasions.

The team was briefly expelled from the league in 2009 when the FAI said that the club had broken regulations by having unofficial secondary contracts with some players. After negotiations, the team was allowed to apply to play in the league's lower division. By 2011, the team were promoted and returned to the premier division.

The club's nickname – The Candystripes – comes from their strip, featuring vertical red and white stripes, similar to the stripes of a candy cane. The club has a strong relationship with its fans and the local community, many of whom came to the team's aid when it became dangerously close to both bankruptcy and relegation in the early 2000s. The current club president is former SDLP leader John Hume.

The Northern Ireland Football League

There are six teams from County Derry competing in the Northern Ireland Football League. Coleraine and Institute (based in Drumahoe) play in the Premiership, while Limavady United, Tobermore United, Moyola Park and Portstewart compete in the lower 'Championship' tiers of the league. There is also a number of smaller teams that compete in the Intermediate league, including Newbuildings United and Draperstown Celtic.

Limavady United

Limavady United have developed a reputation as pranksters. In 2011, the club made headlines around the world after making

Manchester City a cheeky offer to take Argentinian striker Carlos Tevez on loan – a player that City had apparently bought from rivals Manchester United for £47 million.

When Tevez refused to play as a substitute for Manchester City, the Roesiders decided to offer Tevez a chance at regular first team football. Manchester City failed to reply to the offer.

Limavady's midfielder Blain Morrison brought the team into the spotlight again in February 2015. He pretended to be Bolton Wanderers' boss Neil Lennon during a phone call to West Bromwich Albion manager Tony Pulis. Morrison, as Lennon, made a loan bid for Gareth McAuley from Larne. Pulis was completely taken in by the prank, but laughed it off later with the real Neil Lennon during a radio appearance.

Derry has also produced players who play for teams in the British Premier League, such as Darren Gibson who left Manchester United to play for Everton and Wigan Athletic's James McClean. Both players have attracted controversy.

Gibson opted to play for the Republic of Ireland rather than Northern Ireland in 2007. The IFA, the sport's governing body in Northern Ireland, clashed with the FAI, the governing body of the Republic of Ireland, over the issue. However, the IFA were unsuccessful in their bid to prevent Northern Ireland players opting to play for the Republic of Ireland as the matter was settled by the Court of Arbitration for Sport in July 2010.

James McClean was criticised for refusing to wear a poppy on his Sunderland shirt during a match in 2012. McClean said that although he respected the soldiers who had fought in the First and Second World War, he felt the symbol also represented the British soldiers who were responsible for the Bloody Sunday massacre in 1972. McClean received death threats for taking this stance. He has continued to play without the symbol on his shirt for Wigan Athletic and his current club Stoke City.

In February 2014 the pupils and staff at Ampertaine Primary School in Upperlands decided that the entire school would support Premier League football team Aston Villa.

Facts and figures about the team now feature in mathematics, physical education and literacy lessons. The team responded positively to the school and sent the team's mascot Chip the Lion to the school to meet the pupils.

Harry Gregg

Harry Gregg, born in Tobermore, was brought up near the Showgrounds football stadium in Coleraine. He soon realised his abilities as a goalkeeper and at the age of 18 moved to England to join Doncaster Rovers. In December 1957 he signed for Manchester United, then under the command of Matt Busby, for £23,000 which was a world record fee for a goalkeeper at the time.

Not long afterwards, in February 1958, Gregg was among the team returning to Manchester following a match in Belgrade. The plane crashed as it attempted to take off in what became known as the Munich air disaster. Twenty-one people died before the emergency services could arrive at the scene and two more would later die as a result of injury. Eight Manchester United players were among the deceased.

Gregg displayed incredible bravery by helping other passengers out of the burning plane, including a pregnant woman and her baby. He also came to the aid of his teammate Jackie Blanchflower who had been severely injured by using his tie as a tourniquet to stem heavy bleeding from Blanchflower's arm. Gregg himself was only slightly injured and would continue to play on for his team until 1966, making over 200 appearances for the club.

He also played internationally for Northern Ireland and was voted Goalkeeper of the Tournament at the 1958 World Cup in Sweden. He later had a career as a manager with clubs like Swansea City and Shrewsbury Town and was awarded an MBE in 1995.

Martin O'Neill

Martin O'Neill showed promising sporting ability from a young age. He played Gaelic football for Kilrea GAC and progressed to the Derry team that reached the All-Ireland minor semi-final. He missed a penalty that day, allowing Kerry to win by just two points.

O'Neill studied Law at Queen's University, Belfast before making the decision to play professional football. He played for Nottingham Forest, Norwich City and Manchester City and won sixty-four caps for Northern Ireland. He then became a manager and took charge of several prominent teams, including Sunderland, Aston Villa and Celtic.

He was appointed as the manager of the Republic of Ireland team in November 2013, with Roy Keane acting as his assistant. He remained in this role until the end of 2018 and became manager of Nottingham Forest in January 2019.

Milk Cup

The Milk Cup, founded in 1983, has been going strong for over thirty years. Youth football teams come from all around the world to compete on pitches across Antrim and Derry, including those in Coleraine and Limavady.

The tournament has three categories, Junior for Under fourteens, Premier for Under sixteens and Elite for Under nineteens. In addition to national teams, many prestigious teams send their youngsters to compete including Chelsea, Manchester United and Barcelona. Notable players to have played in the tournament include Ryan Giggs, Steve McManaman, Robbie Fowler and David Beckham.

COMBAT SPORTS

Derry has performed strongly in several combat sports. The 2006 Commonwealth Judo Championships were held in Derry's Templemore Sports Complex. Although up against more than 300 competitors from twenty different countries, several of the city's judo players, including Jim Toland and Lisa Bradley, managed to win gold medals at masters level.

Fighters from Derry also perform well in the world of kickboxing. Daniel 'Pinta' Quigley is a four-time world champion in kickboxing at cruiserweight, heavyweight and super heavyweight. Other fighters who have competed on a world level include James Porter and Aidan 'Lights Out' Lafferty.

Most notable among Derry's fighters though, are the boxers that have come from the city and county.

Middleweight John Duddy (29 wins, 2 losses and 0 draws) is perhaps the most famous boxer to come from Derry city in recent years. He made a name for himself as 'The Derry Destroyer' in the United States, fighting mainly in New York. He retired in 2011 having only lost bouts by decision. Since then he has become an actor, appearing in plays and a Bon Jovi video. He played Scottish boxer Ken Buchanan in the film *Hands of Stone* alongside Robert De Niro.

Dungiven is gaining a reputation as the home of great fighters. Paul 'Dudey' McCloskey (24 wins, 3 losses and 0 draws) won the British Light-Welterweight title in his eighteenth fight against Colin Lynes. He had been preparing for a fight on the undercard, but jumped at the chance when Lynes's opponent pulled out. He then won and defended the European title before facing Bolton's Amir Khan for the WBA world title. The fighters clashed heads during the fight, leading McCloskey to be cut. The fight was then stopped, a controversial result that many thought was unjustified. McCloskey retired in 2014 and has since become a barber in Derry's Clarendon Street.

McCloskey's friend from his days at St Canice's ABC in Dungiven also had a successful pro career at middleweight. He won a gold medal for Northern Ireland at the 2010 Commonwealth Games in Delhi, India, beating eventual Olympic medallist Anthony Ogogo in the final. He retired in 2015 with a record of 14 wins, 2 defeats and 1 draw

Derry City's Boxing Dynasties

Jimmy 'Spider' Kelly (121 wins, 34 losses and 12 draws) turned professional in 1928. He won the Featherweight British and Empire belts by defeating Londoner Benny Caplan in November 1938. The fight was held in the King's Hall in Belfast. His victory brought the city together and when he returned he was greeted by a huge crowd and bands from both Nationalist and Unionist areas.

Jimmy's son, Billy (56 wins, 23 losses and 4 draws), would follow his father into boxing under the nickname 'Spider'. He even claimed the same Featherweight British and Empire titles his father had held.

He claimed the Empire title by winning a rematch with Roy Ankrah from Ghana. The October 1954 fight was held in the same venue in which Billy had watched his father win the belt – the King's Hall. He would later revisit Belfast to take the British title from London's Sammy McCarthy in January 1955.

Charlie Nash (25 wins, 5 losses and 0 draws) began boxing in St Mary's Youth Club when he was eleven. Ten years later he would have a year of tremendous highs and lows. He made it to the 1972 Olympics, representing Ireland as a lightweight. Weighing heavily on his mind was the death of his brother, William, who was one of the thirteen men shot dead on Bloody Sunday earlier that year. It is a sad coincidence that losing a relative on that day is something Nash shares with another Derry fighter. The uncle of middleweight John Duddy was also killed on Bloody Sundy. He was also called John and was a boxer himself. He was just 17 when he was shot.

Nash was preparing for his Olympic showdown with Jan Szczepanski, a Pole, when Palestinian paramilitaries launched an attack on the Olympic Village in Munich, killing two Israelis and capturing another nine. When the fight was rescheduled, Nash was knocked out by Szczepanksi, who went on to win the gold medal.

As a professional Nash would win the British and European Lightweight titles before losing in his bid for the WBC World title against Glasgow's Jim Watt. The gloves worn by Nash for this fight can been seen on display in the Tower Museum.

Despite winning the European title in 1979, he only received his belt in 2013, thirty-four years later, when Dungiven's Paul McCloskey and his manager Francie McNicholl managed to buy it from the British Boxing Board of control. Oddly enough, Nash shares his name with a character from the popular game *Street Fighter.*

Roy Nash would later continue the Nash name as an amateur in the 1980s and 1990s. He won a silver medal as a bantamweight at the 1986 Commonwealth Games. He also beat Johnny Tapia as an amateur, who would later become a World Champion in three different weight classes. Roy's son, Callum, is currently making a name for himself as an amateur.

Harry Mullan (1946-1999)

Originally from Portstewart, Mullan moved to London in the 1960s. He began writing as a freelance journalist while working as a civil servant and eventually fulfilled his dream of becoming the editor of *Boxing News* magazine in 1977. He held this position until 1996, wrote several books and contributed to *The Sunday Times* and the *Independent on Sunday.*

He is described as having a great sense of fair play and was committed to making up his own mind, regardless of the hype or controversy surrounding a fight.

He died of cancer aged just fifty-three and was posthumously inducted into the International Boxing Hall of Fame in 2005.

RUGBY

There are two main rugby clubs in the county, City of Derry RFC and Rainey Old Boys RFC in Magherafelt. Both teams play in the All-Ireland league, currently in Division 2A.

Mathematical physicist Thomas Ranken Lyle, from Coleraine, played for Ireland in the 1880s. He competed in three Home Nations Championships, the precursor of the Six Nations. His career was cut short due to a knee injury. He moved to Australia and was a pioneer in X-ray technology. A medal is awarded in his name at the Australian Academy of Science and he has appeared on stamps in his adopted country.

George Beamish, originally from Dunmanway, County Cork, was educated at Coleraine Academical Institution and later was named High Sheriff of County Londonderry. He was an Air Marshal in the RAF during the Second War and fought in the defence of Crete when the island was invaded by the Germans.

He played for Coleraine and Ireland and captained the national team in the 1932 Home Nations Championship. He was selected to play for the British and Irish Lions during their tour of New Zealand in 1930. During this trip, Beamish is said to have been unhappy that Ireland was the only nation not represented by the team's colours – white for England, blue for Scotland and red for Wales. As a result, green was added to the kit and has remained a colour on the strip (often just as part of the crest) ever since.

Coleraine's Andrew Trimble has followed in his footsteps. He has played as a winger for Ulster and Ireland since 2005 and has performed well in World Cup and Six Nations games. He was named Player of the Year for his performance in the 2014 Six Nations tournament by the Rugby Writers of Ireland, but was forced to miss Ireland's defence of the title in 2015 due to a recurring leg injury. Trimble retired in 2018.

CRICKET

There are seven cricket clubs in County Derry, most of which compete in the North West Senior League.

Robert 'Roy' Torrens is perhaps the most recognisable Derry face in cricket. He played for Ireland as a bowler thirty times and later became the team's manager. During his time as manager the team qualified for their first World Cup in 2007 and have competed in two more in 2011 and 2015. He retired in early 2015.

You can easily spot 6ft 8in Boyd Rankin from Derry city who started out at Bready Cricket Club just across the Tyrone border. He has played for Ireland as a bowler seventy-nine times, including World Cup matches. In 2013 he made his debut for the English team and competed in the Ashes series against Australia. In 2016 he returned to the Ireland team and would be part of the Irish team for the country's first ever Test match, against Pakistan in May 2018.

OTHER SPORTS

In September 2009, one of the world's strongest women died suddenly at her home in Upperlands. Trish Porter (38), won the title of UK's Strongest Woman in 2002 and 2003 and was also a runner-up in the 2008 Mr and Mrs Universe competition. Originally from County Wexford, Porter settled in Upperlands with her husband and three children.

The Portstewart Eagles are the only youth baseball team in Northern Ireland. Founded in 1998, the team have competed in contests within the UK, the Republic of Ireland, the United States and in Poland.

Basketball is developing in the county and there are currently two teams, North Star in Derry city and the Magherafelt Titans.

Coleraine's Jenna McCorkell has won the Ladies British Figure Skating Championships eleven times in the twelve competitions from 2003 to 2014. She has also performed well at international competitions, including the 2010 Winter Olympics in Vancouver, Canada and the 2014 games in Sochi, Russia.

In 2014, Derry was part of the route for that year's Clipper Round the World Yacht Race. The city celebrated with the nine-day 'LegenDerry' maritime festival. Highlights of the festival included a continental market and a performance by the Beach Boys at Ebrington Square.

OLYMPIANS

Anton Hegarty won a silver medal at the 1920 Antwerp Olympics. Despite being wounded in the First World War, Hegarty continued to run as a member of Derry City Harriers athletics club. He competed as a member of the British cross-country team, at a time when Ireland could not compete as a country in the games.

Wendy Houvenaghel from Upperlands, near Maghera, represented Britain as a cyclist at many major events. Among her achievements are a silver medal in the 2008 Beijing Olympic Games and three World Championships.

She was controversially left out of the British team pursuit team that won gold medals at the 2012 Olympics, setting a world record time. She was critical of her coach's decision to leave her out of all three races, when competing in just one would have made her eligible for a medal. She retired in July 2014, after an injury forced her to withdraw from that year's Commonwealth Games.

Alan Campbell, a rower from Coleraine, won several medals at World Rowing Championships in the single sculls event. He competed in the same event in the 2008 Beijing Olympics, finishing fifth. At the 2012 Olympics, Campbell won a bronze medal for Great Britain – the country's first in single sculls for nearly ninety years.

Campbell's friends at the Bann Rowing Club, brothers Richard and Peter Chambers, have represented Britain on the world stage on many occasions, as members of the British teams for the Lightweight Pairs and Men's Four events.

The brothers from Coleraine have both been members of teams which won gold medals at the World Championships, Peter in 2011 in Bled, Slovenia and Richard in 2007 in Munich, Germany and again in 2010 in Karapiro, New Zealand.

They were both members of the British lightweight men's four team that won silver medals at the 2012 London Olympics.

PARALYMPIANS

Jason Smyth is a sprinter from Eglinton. As he is legally blind, he competes as an athlete in the Paralympic Games. 'He has won five gold paralympics medals competing in the 100m and 200m races at the Olympics in Beijing in 2008, London in 2012 and Rio De Janeiro in 2016.

Although he set new world records for both events at the 2012 games, he had also hoped to compete in the 2012 Olympic Games but just missed out on the time needed to qualify.

Sally Brown from Ballykelly was born with dysmelia in her left arm, which meant that it did not develop below her elbow. She has won medals in the 100m and 200m sprint at the IWAS World Junior Championships and competed in the 100m sprint at the 2012 Paralympics in London, where she finished sixth.

In addition to celebrating Olympians in their midst, the citizens of Derry were able to see the Olympic torch for themselves as it passed through the county in the build-up to the 2012 London Olympics.

Sixty locals were chosen to be torch bearers as the torch travelled through Coleraine, Articlave, Castlerock, Limavady, Ballykelly and

Greysteel before arriving in Derry city. The relay ended for the day when the torch was taken across the Peace Bridge and used to ignite a cauldron.

THE NORTH WEST 200

The motorcycle race known as the North West 200 is regarded as one of the fastest of its kind in the world, with speeds sometimes exceeding 200mph. It runs on public roads between Coleraine and Portstewart in County Derry and Portrush in County Antrim.

The race was dominated by brothers Robert and Joey Dunlop for many years, winning a combined twenty-eight times – fifteen for Robert and thirteen for Joey. Both brothers died in accidents, Joey when he lost control of his bike and collided with a tree in 2000. Robert died after suffering severe chest injuries following a crash during a practice session for the 2008 North West 200.

Robert's sons now represent the family name at the event. Michael Dunlop won the 2008 250cc race, the event his father had been practising for when he died. William Dunlop won the same event the next year, while both brothers won races in 2014.

The event attracts a crowd of over 100,000 annually and in recent years it is claimed that more than two million people across the world have tuned into the races.

8

THIS, THAT AND THE OTHER

This is the final chapter. I know there must be at least few who have nodded and yawned as page after page you've read facts and stories you've known inside out for years. Nobody can tell you some new odd fact about Derry, says you. Well you're dead wrong.

These are the pay-off pages for the fact hungry, the one-man-uppers, the fiendish pub quizmasters and the wide-eyed small town dreamers who want to see oddities swim up from outside their window.

WORLD RECORDS

January 1996 – Eamonn McGirr left Derry for New York where he gained a reputation as a man who could raise vast amounts of money for charity. He broke the world record for marathon singing after carrying a tune for eleven days and twenty minutes. His efforts raised thousands of dollars for the disabled in Albany, New York, including his daughter Mareena who suffers from cerebral palsy. Sadly, a fall caused McGirr to become paralysed from the chest down just months after breaking the record and he died in 2004.

December 2007 – In what is believed to be the first world record attempt in Northern Ireland, 13,000 Christmas lovers took part in a charity event on Derry's walls. The crowd broke the world record for the 'Largest gathering of people dressed as Santa Claus'. However, this record was beaten by a crowd of 18,112 Santas in Kerala, India, on 27 December 2014.

December 2009 – 100 volunteers, including Nadine Coyle of *Girls Aloud*, set a new world record for the number of trees planted in one hour. The event was organised by Conversation Volunteers Northern Ireland (CVNI) as part of National Tree Week. The team planted 26,422 trees in the grounds of Gransha hospital, beating the previous record of 18,124 by a long way.

March 2013 – Over 5,480 people gathered in Ebrington Square to perform the song and dance routine from the musical *Annie*. Adjudicator Martin Mullan announced the crowd had smashed the previous record of 4,500 performers of this song and dance.

April 2013 – Between 750 and 800 women took part in the 'Brides across the Bridge' record attempt. People came from all over, dressed in full bridal wear, to cross the city's Peace Bridge and set the record. Participants included 91-year-old Sheila Cooper, along with Sinita Duffy, who took a break from celebrating her own wedding day to take part.

August 2013 – Dancers at Derry City's Fleadh Cheoil na hÉireann smashed the world record for 'Longest *Riverdance* line' that had been set only a month before in Dublin. Nearly 1,700 dancers lined out in Dublin, but they were easily outdone by more than 2,500 people who endured heavy rain to take the title in Ebrington Square.

September 2014 – Pupils from Derry and Donegal celebrated breaking the Guinness World Record for 'Most Signatures on a Scroll'. The group managed to obtain 14,000 signatures for their 'Peace Pledge' initiative, beating the previous record of 10,000. The attempt aimed to raise awareness for the International Day of Peace in 2014.

ANNIE LONDONDERRY

Annie Londonderry (1870-1947) was setting world records more than fifty years before Guinness even starting recording them. She was born Annie Cohen Kopchovsky in Riga, Latvia and moved to the United States as a child.

When she was twenty-three she made a wager with some Boston businessmen that she could cycle around the world in fifteen months, earning $5,000 on the way. Although she had never ridden a bicycle before, she grabbed some clothes and a 'pearl-handled' revolver before leaving her husband and three young children behind. She travelled from Boston to New York, from there she passed through France and cycled on to Egypt, Jersualem and Singapore. She returned to San Francisco and passed through Los Angeles, El Paso and Denver before arriving home in Boston, 15 months after she left.

She became famous as the first woman to cycle around the world. Her feat and attitude challenged stuffy Victorian conventions of how a woman should dress and act and it is believed that she had an influence on the Suffragette movement.

Her nickname derives from the fact that the Londonderry Lithia Spring Water Company, based in Londonderry, New Hampshire, paid her to advertise their product around the world, carrying banners on her bike.

County Derry woman Bridget Young followed in Annie's tracks in September 1927. At the age of 20 she set a record for woman motor-cyclists by motorcycling 1000 miles in five days.

TWO CENTENARIANS OF CASTLEDAWSON

Ordnance Survey Memoirs from 1836 state that Castledawson man John Hillman died in 1821 at the age of 115. If verified, this would make him the oldest person to ever live in Ireland and a close second to the United Kingdom record holder. It is reported that he would go out horse riding every morning without fail, even when he passed 100 and could travel up to thirty miles daily.

A newspaper article revealed the simple life of Archibald Williamson, who died in 1921 at the age of 100. It stated that in a century of life the Castledawson man was never – even just for a walk – more than five miles away from where he was born, except for one occasion where he drove some cattle to a fair in Cookstown, 10 miles away. The paper reported that he never saw the sea and was never in a train, despite living close to three stations.

THE
DERRY JOURNAL

The *Derry Journal* has a complicated and controversial history and has, over the years, been banned on both sides of the border – but not at the same time. The paper was founded in 1772, which makes it one of Ireland's oldest newspapers, perhaps second only to Belfast's *News Letter* which was founded in 1737.

It was originally a Unionist paper until it endorsed Catholic Emancipation in 1829, a move that lead the editor to resign and found a rival paper, the *Londonderry Sentinel*. Since then, it has been regarded as a paper with generally Nationalist leanings.

Following the partition of Ireland, the *Derry Journal* was critical of the Cumman na nGaedheal government, which was in power from 1923 to 1933. On 1 January 1932 the paper's editorial encouraged readers in the Irish Free State to vote for the 'right' party – Fianna Fáil – in the upcoming elections. A few days later copies of the paper were confiscated in Donegal and newsagents were told by Gardaí that no copies were to be sold until official permission was given.

The paper was free to cover its own banning in Northern Ireland and expressed frustration and confusion at the events. Investigating the ban with the authorities, they were unable to find out who authorised and organised the ban, which was quickly rescinded.

Following the outbreak of the Second World War, the paper declared a neutral stance, in keeping with the attitude of Eamon de Valera's free state government. Although the paper took pains to stress that their neutrality did not mean they supported the Nazis, the Stormont government saw fit to ban the paper on 1 June 1940.

The ban was supposed to run until the end of the year, but was revoked after just four days. As the *Derry Journal* was published three times a week, the ban meant only one issue was not published in Northern Ireland. As before, the paper was able to cover its own ban, this time in its Donegal edition.

DERRY AND BEYOND!

The Bovedy Meteorite
A fireball was seen travelling west 'extremely rapidly' in the sky in over Sussex, Yorkshire and later Belfast on 25 April 1969. Further sightings were later reported from Donegal, Down and Fermanagh.

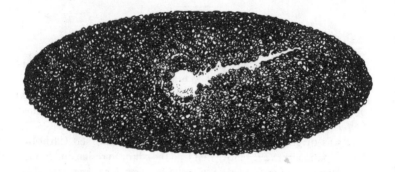

It was also seen by a Mr A. Cuddy of Dublin, who managed to record a precise time for his sighting, as it interrupted a greyhound race he was watching at the time. Witnesses in Wales described the meteorite as being 'blue green' and reported a double sonic boom.

A piece of the meteorite fell through the roof of an RUC station in Sprucefield, but the largest piece, weighing 4.95kg, landed in a field in Bovedy, near Kilrea, and gave the meteorite its name.

It is one of the few meteorites in the world that was recorded and can be heard today. A woman happened to be recording birds singing just as the meteorite crashed to earth. The audio she recorded is kept by the Armagh Planetarium.

Other Meteorites

There are very few records of meteorites falling anywhere in Ireland. However, most of these few appear to have some association with Derry. In addition to the Bovedy meteorite, the records also state that several 'aerolites' fell at Killeter, in 1844.

In February 2010, a man driving on the Glenshane Pass described seeing a fireball which was 'very bright green and with an orange tail'.

'It was travelling at fantastic speed, very high up in the sky,' said Joss Scott. 'It then went behind these black clouds over the Sperrins, towards Dungiven, then there was this large orange flash, so I'm not sure if it landed somewhere around there.'

No remains or impact crater have been found to date for this meteorite, which experts think may have crashed in Donegal, Cavan, Armagh or even into Lough Neagh. However, if you live in Dungiven or nearby, it might be worth your while to have a wee look around the garden. The last meteorite to land in Ireland was sold online in 1999 for over £300 per gram!

DERRY IN FICTION

Owen Sleater, a character in HBO's *Boardwalk Empire*, was an immigrant from Coleraine. He becomes the driver and bodyguard of Nucky Thompson (Steve Buscemi) and an important part of his criminal organisation in New Jersey.

Alfred Bester's 1956 book *The Stars My Destination* features a man named Gulliver Foyle as the main character. Bester used place names from Ireland and the UK to come up with names for characters, including Saul Dagenham and Regis Sheffield.

In the TV series *Elementary*, Sherlock Holmes (Jonny Lee-Miller) is seen practising his Derry accent. Watson (Lucy Liu) is a bit confused but says she's sure the accent would come in useful if he ever had to go undercover in the city!

TRANSPORT

The train journey from Derry to Belfast, which incorporates Coleraine and the north coast, was described as 'one of the most beautiful rail journeys in the world' by Michael Palin. However, the train service between the two cities was criticised in June 2014, when cyclist John Madden managed to beat his friend Peter Jack, who took the train, in a race from a post office in Derry to one in Belfast.

Downhill tunnel near Magilligan was created in 1846. The blasting of the tunnel was a popular event that attracted a crowd of more than 12,000 people. When the dust settled, an extravagant banquet was then held in the new tunnel.

THE DUNGIVEN COSTUME

In 1956 farmers near Dungiven uncovered some clothes in a field. The 'Dungiven Costume' consisted of a cloak, jacket, trousers and some leather brogues.

The costume has been dated to the late 1600s and is believed to have once been elaborately coloured. The clothes were said to have been well made when new, but had been patched several times over the years. Their size suggested a rather large man, as the jacket was made for a 42-inch chest.

You can view the original Dungiven costume and a reconstruction in the Ulster Museum. Better still, as the tartan design was registered with an American company, you can buy your very own authentic replica of the costume.

BUSINESS

Ice Cream

The residents of County Derry definitely have a sweet tooth, as the area is known for producing top quality ice cream. Mullin's ice cream was founded in 1954 and now produces ice cream for over fifty scoop parlours across Northern Ireland from its factory in Kilrea.

Morelli's ice cream is also well established in Portstewart. Their first shop in the town, The Ice Palace, opened in 1929 and was run by Angelo Morelli.

During the Second World War, the Morelli family was split up. Angelo was interned in a camp on the Isle of Man and was to be deported to Canada, but was taken off the ship just before it sailed. The ship was attacked by a German U-boat and sank, with no survivors. His sons Nino and Corrado had gone to Italy before the war broke out and fled their home when the Allied forces arrived in Italy.

By a stroke of luck, an army officer from Portstewart knew the Morelli name, he made sure the boys were looked after and helped them return to Ireland in 1945. The company now has shops across Northern Ireland, selling flavours like blackcurrant and liquorice, sea salty caramel and parma violet.

Nestlé

Nestlé opened a plant in Castledawson in 1943. Using milk from counties Derry and Tyrone, it produced millions of gallons of sweetened condensed milk, which was exported to places around the world. Although very popular during the Second World War, demand for the product fell and the plant was closed in 1980.

Ditty's

Ditty's Bakery in Castledawson won a contract in 2011 to supply shortbread to Irish and UK expatriates based in the Middle East and North Africa. Some of their products can also be found in China.

DuPont

The DuPont factory at Maydown is one of only four plants producing Kevlar, and the only one in Europe. The material is used in construction and electronics but is best known as a major component of body armour, used by military and police forces across the world.

Stars of The Apprentice

In 2013, Dr Leah Totton from the Waterside was a contestant on the BBC Television reality show *The Apprentice*. She eventually won the series, and received a £250,000 prize from Lord Alan Sugar to invest in a business. In 2014, she opened her first cosmetic surgery, the Dr Leah Cosmetic Skin Clinic in London. She was in the news again later that year when she came to the aid of a man who collapsed in Liverpool Street railway station.

James McCullough, a pupil of Loreto College Coleraine, appeared on the version of the show for teenagers, *The Young Apprentice*, in 2011. He came second in the contest, just missing out on a £25,000 prize from Lord Sugar.

NUCLEAR DERRY

In 1987 Lord Lyell, the agriculture minister, announced that tests performed on sheep from the Glenshane Pass showed they had dangerously high levels of radiation. He then banned the movement and slaughter of these animals, putting them into 'nuclear quarantine'. This restriction would not be fully lifted until 2000.

It turns out this was a result of fallout from the 1986 nuclear explosion in Chernobyl, Ukraine. Contaminated rain fell in the Derry area in the days following the disaster. Some people in the area believe that the radiation in the air at the time may have led to an increase in cancer cases.

However, this is not the only link between County Derry and nuclear disaster. After the Second World War forty-four bunkers were built across Northern Ireland to monitor the threat of nuclear attacks from Russia.

Plans were drawn up for an attack on Northern Ireland by the Russians during the Cold War. A report released by the Russian Government in 2006 revealed that ten nuclear warheads had been aimed at Northern Ireland throughout the Cold War. Their targets included airports, but also Ballykelly army barracks and former US naval facilities at Lisahally.

The Sperrins were also a target, as it was believed US Navy transmitters were based there.

RELIGIOUS CONCERNS

Halloween is a big event in Derry city. The annual carnival and fireworks draws up to 30,000 spooks, ghouls, monsters and witches to the city for a night of family fun.

However, not everyone is so impressed with the party. In 2009, Revd Jonathan Campbell, an Independent Methodist minister, called on families to boycott the celebrations. He claimed that although Halloween seems like harmless fun, it is in fact 'one of the major days for Satanists'. He said that 'Christians believe that evil is a real but defeated power. Halloween however, is evil triumphant, therefore it is a distortion of reality. This carnival brings a curse upon the city.' He set up an online petition to call on Derry City Council to ban the carnival, which only attracted 189 signatories.

A Catholic priest expressed similar concerns in February 2015 when he said that practising yoga or getting an Indian head massage would lead people to Satanism and the 'Kingdom of Darkness'. Father Ronald Colhoun, based in the Waterside, made the comments while saying mass. His remarks made news worldwide and deeply offended many Hindus. A group based in Nevada, USA even urged Pope Francis to step in and discipline the priest.

NATURAL DISASTERS AND THE WEATHER

The San Franciso Earthquake

Henry Walls from Ballymaguigan was living in San Francisco in 1906 when an earthquake measuring 7.8 on the Richter scale devastated the city. It is believed that 3,000 people died in the chaos following the disaster and fires 'that burned for four days' destroyed many of the buildings.

He wrote a letter home to his mother and brother in Ireland describing the catastrophe. He talks about a friend who worked on a lumber ship. He took a room in a hotel, but after being disturbed by a drunk, left and went to his ship instead. The next morning, the hotel and its forty-two inhabitants had sunk into the earth. Another hotel containing 200 'ladies of easy virtue' met a similar fate.

His stories depict the chaos after the disaster. For example, he speaks about a lady who jumped out of bed, grabbed her pug under one arm and a canary's cage under the other and set off down the street. In her confusion she did not notice that the cage was empty and she was wearing little more than a bonnet.

The Eglinton Tornado

In June 2011 ten men were working on a farm near Eglinton when what they described as a tornado struck. The roof was ripped off a barn and hurled into the air, while a wall collapsed onto a car, destroying it. The men were shaken but unharmed by the incident.

The local BBC weather presenter Cecilia Daly said that a tornado was not out of the question given the conditions in the area at the time. However, she felt it was more likely that the damage was caused by a 'downburst' which is not as powerful as a tornado but still formidable.

Winter in Derry

The Glenshane Pass was hit by a severe snowstorm in March 2010, which caused snowdrifts over a metre high to block the pass at both

sides. A rescue operation had to be organised by mountain rescue, the coastguard and the PSNI to evacuate around 300 people from over 120 trapped vehicles.

In January 2015, an 18-year-old from Park became famous around the world. Ruairi McSorley spoke to UTV about the cold weather, telling the journalist that in the icy conditions 'You wouldn't be long getting frostbit.' This clip of 'Frostbit boy' became a viral sensation as millions of people around the world were intrigued by his accent and mannerisms.

ANIMALS

Gorgeous

A farmer from Garvagh credits the beauty of his British Blue cow, Gorgeous, for his marriage. Steven O'Kane met Katrina Donaldson, from Yorkshire, when she wanted to buy the cow. Steven agreed to sell Gorgeous on condition that he could take Katrina on a date!

The couple married in May 2014. Gorgeous could not attend the ceremony, but is said to have been the star of the reception.

Dog Leap

On a visit to Binevanagh mountain near Limavady, German pointer Rover took the region's name a little too literally, when he plunged nearly 400 feet off a cliff. The dog was brought home to Scotland where vets worked on his injuries. Although Rover's organs and bones were relatively undamaged, he had damaged two vertebrae.

His owners needed thousands of pounds to pay for the treatment. Generous donors managed to give half of the money, meaning that Rover had an operation the following week.

Wolves

A fire broke out and destroyed Edward Randolph's settlement at Derry in 1567. It was believed that an accident in a blacksmith's forge was the cause and an explosion in the ammunition store intensified the flames. However, some more superstitious people said that the fire was the work of a monstrous wolf. It was described as being 'of huge size and with bristling hair' and emerged from the woods to set the ammunition store alight with sparks from its mouth.

It is believed that the last wolf in Ireland was killed in 1786 in County Carlow. However, this claim is disputed by several stories from Derry.

A Bishop of Derry recalled a conversation he had with a Mr Duncan of Dungiven in the 1830s. He said that he met Duncan when was quite old and that the man had spoken of a wolf being executed on a nearby hill when he was young. Another account supports this story, saying that a wolf was sighted at Benevenagh and tracked to woods near Dungiven where it was killed. Similar stories of Ireland's last wolf can also be found in Cluntygeragh and Craigashoke near Draperstown and Glenconkeyne. However, it is unlikely that any of these stories, including the Carlow one, can ever be properly verified.

THE WEIRD
AND WONDERFUL

St Columba's Voyage

The legend of St Columba is that in AD 563 he sailed to the island of Iona in Scotland in a wooden boat covered with animal hides, known as a currach. He was accompanied by twelve monks and together they set up a monastery on the island.

In 1963, 1,400 years after Columba's voyage, thirteen men recreated the journey. They left Derry in a similar currach to the one Columba might have used and arrived on the island in eight days. The 30-foot boat they used is now on display in Derry's Harbour Museum.

Cruithne

The Cruithne were once powerful warriors in counties Antrim, Down and Derry in the fourth and fifth centuries. Not only do they give their name to local areas – Drumcroon near Coleraine means 'hill of the Cruithne' – but an asteroid discovered in 1986, 3753 Cruithne, was also named after them.

This asteroid became quite famous after it was described as the Earth's 'second moon' on the BBC Television series *QI*. However, some scientists have argued that Cruithne is a near-Earth satellite and does not qualify as a moon.

Derry Cuisine

Following waves of immigration, Americans began to hold lavish banquets to mark St Patrick's Day in the nineteenth century. Then, as today, the cuisine was deemed to be improved by translating its name into French. So, instead of tucking into some mashed spuds you were presented with 'pommes de terre persillade'.

A strange menu from 1919 opens with 'Grapefruit Irlandaise' and a mysterious soup called 'Potage Londonderry'. There is no record of the recipe, or what the dish contained, but as Derry has never produced a thick soup distinctive enough to carry its name, perhaps it is best forgotten.

Everest

In 2007, Hannah Shields, a dentist from Kilrea, became the first woman from Northern Ireland to climb Mount Everest.

The first Irish woman to reach the summit was Dr Clare O'Leary from Cork, who reached the top in May 2004. Shields was close to taking this title herself in a May 2003 expedition, but had to turn back near the summit due to extreme weather and frostbite. The first Irish person to reach the top was Dawson Stelfox from Belfast in 1993.

COUNTY DERRY SUPERSTITIONS

Banagher sand is revered for its supposed lucky qualities. It has been said that you need only throw some sand from Banagher on a jockey to ensure the success of his horse, or carry some into court in your pocket to guarantee victory in a legal dispute.

It was once common in the county to bury Catholic priests with their shoes on, sometimes paved with nails in order to 'carry them safe through the firey trial of purgatory'.

Hearing a cock crowing at an unusual hour was once taken as a bad omen that someone in the family would die within a year – but only if its legs were cold. If the cock's legs were warm then it was believed that a member of family would travel far in the direction the cock was facing within the next year.

Young Catholic women would try to learn about their future husbands by placing a snail into a clean metal pot and closing it up for the night. In the morning they expected to find that the snail had written the name of the man they would marry.

BITS AND BOBS

In 1962, Hugh Robinson (29) was carrying a ladder at a Derry power station when it touched an overhead cable. He got a shock of 110,000 volts, which caused his rubber boots to melt against his legs. His employer said that he would have been killed instantly if it was not for the boots and the wooden ladder. Instead, he was said to be merely 'ill' in hospital.

There is said to be a network of tunnels under Limavady, yet nobody knows what purpose they are supposed to serve. Suggestions put forward include the idea that the tunnels were used to store whiskey in cool conditions, or that it was a place to *hide* whiskey, or that the tunnels were there to allow residents to escape if the town came under attack.

The skeleton seen on Derry city's arms is that of Walter de Burgo, a Norman knight who was thrown into a dungeon by his own cousin and left to starve in 1332.

Derry natives have long held the local oak trees in high regard. Certain taboos were attached to them by Celtic pagans, some of which carried over to Christians when that faith became established. According to records from 1188, a man cutting firewood from these trees violated some ancient rule and was suddenly killed by 'a miracle of Colmcille'.

Shipquay Street in Derry city was transformed into a giant three-lane slide in September 2014. Some 1,600 enjoyed the slide, donating money to Cancer Research for the opportunity.

Michael Flatley, 'The Lord of the Dance', is said to have danced in Dungiven Castle during a visit to Ireland in the 1980s.

Twins Anthony and Annie McGroarty, who lived in the Culmore area, were born in different decades. The circumstances of their birth were investigated after their birth certificates were presented when enrolling the children in school. It was then discovered that Annie was registered as having been born at 11.30p.m. on 31 December 1939 and Thomas was born an hour later at 12.30a.m. on 1 January 1940.

An odd newspaper article from October 1903 relates the story of a Draperstown man in his '70s who was preparing to remarry. Yet, determined to stop the wedding, his daughter and her husband broke into his home on the morning of the big day and hid his clothing. The man went about his business regardless and it was reported that he found some 'scanty wearing apparel' got married and soon after the ceremony ensured his daughter and son-in-law were arrested.

A letter from a woman in Magherafelt to her son in England took 45 years to be delivered. In 1873 she posted the letter to Joseph McKenna in Liverpool. It was misplaced and was eventually found in 1918, faded with age and down the back of an old desk. The message was then sent back to Magherafelt and given to Mr McKenna, whose mother had passed away 20 years earlier.

In 1904 it was reported that a village in County Derry contained 13 dwellings, 11 of which were pubs. The other two were a creamery and what must have been a very busy police station.

BIBLIOGRAPHY

BOOKS AND ARTICLES

Bartlett, Douglas, *An Illustrated History of Limavady and the Roe Valley from Prehistoric to Modern Times* (Douglas Bartlett, 2010)

Beckett, J.C., *The Making of Modern Ireland 1603–1923* (Faber & Faber, 1981).

Chamlee, Roy, *Lincoln's Assassins: A Complete Account of Their Capture, Trial and Punishment* (McFarland & Co., 2009).

Curran, Bob, *Dark Fairies* (New Page Books, 2010).

Curran, Bob, 'The Problem with Poltergeists', *Ghosts, Specters and Haunted Places*, Michael Pye and Kirsten Dalley (eds) (New York: Rosen Publishing Group, 2013), pp. 43-65.

Curran, Bob, *The World's Creepiest Places* (Career Press, 2012).

Curran, Bob, *Across the Roe: From Bann to Faughan* (Cottage Publications, 2006).

Diner, Hasia, *Hungering for America – Italian, Irish and Jewish Foodways in the Age of Migration* (Harvard University Press, 2001).

Doherty, Richard, *The Siege of Derry 1689: The Military History* (Spellmount, 2008).

Donnelly, E. (ed.), *Moneyneena – A Hundred Years* (2002).

Duffy, Sean, *Medieval Ireland: An Encyclopedia* (Taylor & Francis, 2004).

Fitzgerald, Patrick and Lambkin, Brian, *Migration in Irish History, 1607–2007* (Palgrave Macmillan, 2008).

FitzPatrick, Elizabeth, *Royal Inauguration in Gaelic Ireland c.1100–1600* (Boydell Press, 2004).

Forristal, Desmond, *Colum Cille – The Fox and the Dove*, (Veritas Publications, 1997).

Gébler, Carlo, *The Siege of Derry – A History* (Abacus, 2006).

Gibson, Kenneth, *Killer Doctors – The Ultimate Betrayal of Trust* (Neil Wilson Publishing, 2013).

Hickey, Kieran, *Deluge: Ireland's Weather Disasters 2009–2010* (Four Courts Press, 2010).

Hickey, Kieran, *Wolves in Ireland: A Natural and Cultural History* (Four Courts Press, 2011).

Hughes, Matthew,*The Banality of Brutality: British Armed Forces and the Repression of the Arab Revolt in Palestine, 1936-39*, Brunel University, 2009, retrived from http://v-scheiner.brunel.ac.uk/bitstream/2438/7251/4/The%20banality%20of%20brutality.pdf

Kelly, Richie, *Sporting Greats of the North West* (Guildhall Press, 2011).

Lacey, Brian, *Discover Derry* (Guildhall Press, 1999).

Lacey, Brian, *Medieval and Monastic Derry – Sixth Century to 1600* (Four Courts Press, 2013).

Loughrey, S.V.P. (ed.), *Ordnance Survey Memoir for the Parish of Ballinascreen* (Ballinascreen Historical Society, 1981).

McClements, Freya, *Press Censorship and Emergency Rule in Ireland: The Ban on the Derry Journal, 1932 & 1940* (Master's thesis, 2005), Dublin City University, retrieved from www.dcu.ie/communications/FMC_thesis.pdf.

McCormack, Ken, *Ken McCormack's Derry* (Londubh Books, 2010).

Ó Baoill, Ruairi, *Island City – The Archaeology of Derry-Londonderry* (Northern Ireland Environment Agency and Derry City Council, 2013).

Richardson, H. (ed.), *Ordnance Survey Memoirs for the Parishes of Desertmartin and Kilcronaghan 1836-1837* (Ballinascreen Historical Society, 1986).

Richardson, Neil, *A Coward if I Return, A Hero if I Fall – Stories of Irishmen in World War I*, (O'Brien Press, 2010).

Room, Adrian, *Dictionary of Irish Place Names* (Appletree Press, 2009).

Sheane, Michael, *Famine in the Land of Ulster* (Arthur H. Stockwell Ltd. 2008).

WEBSITES

www.belfasttelegraph.co.uk
http://billhaneman.ie/
www.derryjournal.com

www.historyireland.com
www.irishnews.com
www.londonderrysentinel.co.uk
www.placenamesni.org
www.ulsterbiography.co.uk
www.ulsterhistory.co.uk